Fountains in the Dust

Fountains in the Dust

Snapshots from the Streets of South America

Adrian Plass, Bridget Plass and Angela Murray

14 13 12 11 10 09 08   7 6 5 4 3 2 1

First published 2008 by Authentic Media
9 Holdom Avenue, Bletchley, Milton Keynes, Bucks, MK1 1QR, UK
1820 Jet Stream Drive, Colorado Springs, CO 80921, USA
Medchal Road, Jeedimetla Village, Secunderabad 500 055, A.P., India
www.authenticmedia.co.uk

Authentic Media is a division of IBS-STL U.K., limited by guarantee, with its Registered
Office at Kingstown Broadway, Carlisle, Cumbria CA3 0HA. Registered in England & Wales
No. 1216232. Registered charity 270162

British Library Cataloguing in Publication Data
A catalogue record for this book is available from the British Library

ISBN-13: 978-1-85078-817-1

Photographs taken by Matt Wenham, David Withers, Angela Murray, Marco Patino and
Bridget Plass – used with permission. All photos included in this book were taken with
permission and present a true and fair representation of Toybox's work with the children of
Latin America. Please note that the names of the children and young people featured in this
book may have been changed for their own safety and protection. Toybox has a child
protection policy in place and our overseas partners work with the projects we support to
ensure child protection procedures are followed.

Cover Design by fourninezero design.
Print Management by Adare
Printed and bound in Great Britain by Bell & Bain Ltd., Glasgow

Acknowledgements

**Adrian, Bridget and Ange
would like to thank**

The Viva International team who looked
after us so well in South America,
especially Dennis, Daniel, Ines and
Yerko.

All the project leaders who welcomed us
so warmly, and shared their dreams and
visions with us.

Katya, our wonderful translator.

The children of South America – as this
book shows, we learnt so much from
you and we so enjoyed meeting you.

David Withers, Matt Wenham and Carys
Alford for being part of our travelling
team.

Marco Patino, David Withers and Matt
Wenham for the use of their photos.

Contents

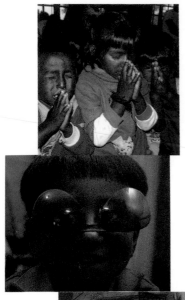

Ange

 My name is Angela Murray, Ange for short, and most of the time I get up in the mornings expecting just another standard day in the office. Sometimes, though, I wake up knowing that the day ahead is likely to be anything but ordinary. As I prepared to meet my travelling companions at Heathrow airport, I was sure that the next two weeks would be packed full of new experiences, new challenges and new adventures.

As part of our work within the staff team at Toybox, Carys Alford and I had been tasked with the job of taking a small group of people to South America. Adrian and Bridget Plass were coming to see the work with the street children for themselves, and their experiences and thoughts were to be captured on film by our two travelling cameramen: David Withers and Matt Wenham.

I'd planned the trip in as much detail as I could. There was the DVD to film, overseas partners to meet and encourage, workshops to run and reports to write. But those were just the written aims. Behind all that were the things I was really worried about. Could I keep everyone safe? Would my Spanish be good enough? Would this thrown-together group of people manage to get on with each other for a whole two weeks? Of course, the existence of this book suggests that we did manage to make it home and remain friends!

Looking back at our travels, it's not the work I had to do which I remember. It's the people I met and the stories I heard which are engraved on my memory. It may have been just two short weeks but a part of me knows that, even if it's just in small ways, life will never be the same.

Adrian

 My name is Adrian Plass. For the last twenty years I have been passing my confusion about the Christian faith on to others through books, talks and Bible notes. Sometimes my confusion eases, usually when I come across a Christian or group of Christians who are actually doing stuff.

In the sixties and seventies we were so worried about doing things in our own strength that we very often ended up doing nothing at all. Since then I have begun to understand that we are called to work as hard as we can for others and for God until, inevitably, we reach the edge of our personal chasm of inadequacy. At that point we have no choice but to rely on the Holy Spirit to construct the supernatural bridge that will get us to the other side. Elijah was devastated by fear whenever the Spirit was not actually operating in his life. In contrast, Daniel was much more impressive as a personality: very committed, very organized, very highly principled. When it came to Nebuchadnezzar's dreams, however, Daniel would have been helpless without direct and detailed information from God.

Work hard and let God do the things that only he can do. That seems to be the way to go. Toybox and their partners in Peru, Bolivia and Guatemala are working hard to improve the lives of street children in Latin America, and they pray constantly that God will support them and fill in the gaps.

Travelling to Peru and Bolivia with a Toybox team was exciting, alarming, exhilarating, uncomfortable, funny, tragic, wearisome and inspiring for Bridget and me. We met so many heroic Christians who will never be famous in this world, but who are already stars in the next. This book is a chance for you to meet some of them and lots of the children they care for, to go to some of the amazing places we visited and to share experiences that were vividly unforgettable.

I do hope you enjoy travelling with us.

Bridget

 My name is Bridget Plass, and I felt like the Gideon of the group: indisputably the least of the least. I could speak no Spanish, was not employed by Toybox, had an extremely hazy idea about what we were going to do, and felt totally inadequate. I am now going to let you into a shameful secret: I didn't even know where Bolivia was until I looked it up on the map!

In the weeks leading up to our departure I became very nervous. Express kidnapping (being marched to a cashpoint and forced to withdraw and hand over money), riots on the streets, rabid dogs – was there no end to the bad stuff in the country we were going to? I didn't know then that travelling with Angela, Carys, Dave and Matt was to be a genuinely funny, warm and affirming experience, or that our hosts in both Peru and Bolivia would be the sweetest, kindest, most hospitable folk on the planet.

And then of course there were the children. Come and meet them with us – I think you'll like them!

BRIEFINGS:
Children Living on the Streets

There are estimated to be around eight hundred children living on the streets of Lima.

Many street children originate from families living in extreme poverty. Others have run away from violence or abuse. Some street children are orphans, whilst an increasing number are part of street families and were born on the streets.

Street children have to survive by their wits. Working, begging and stealing typically form part of their daily lives.

Most street children are addicted to drugs, the most common being glue-sniffing.

If I Were God I Wouldn't Let the Children Die

If I were God I wouldn't let the children die
Not me, I'd use my power
Wouldn't you?
You'd never find me sitting round in heaven
Twiddling my eternal thumbs
As some poor baby fades to nothing
Wailing for a love that never comes
I'd get my act together, heal some pain
Hurl some thunder
Send some rain
Clothe some orphans
Dig some wells
Throw some parties
Ring some bells
Feed some kids
Win some fights
Build some homes
Fly some kites
That's what I would do
I'd look for helpers who would be my hands and feet
They'd show my face in every slum and street
They'd broadcast love and let compassion fly
That's what I would do if I were God
I wouldn't let the children die
Would you?

Adrian Plass

Give a Sunday for a street child

Your church + 10 minutes = changed lives!

Sign up now for your free Sunday for a street child DVD, which includes:

- An exclusive short video presentation by Adrian and Bridget Plass recorded live in Latin America
- A talk delivered by Mark Melluish, New Wine Leader (video and notes)
- Devotional worship presentation (music & images)
- Sunday for a Street Child poster graphics
- Sunday for a Street Child introductory PowerPoint presentation
- Sunday for a Street Child introductory paragraph for your notices
- Child Ambassador Scheme forms

Can we challenge your church to change lives this year?

To bring about change in the lives of street children in Latin America we would like you to find a few minutes space in one of your services this autumn to highlight the work of Toybox in your church.

What does it involve?

If you think your church could spare just 10 minutes we'll send you a Toybox Sunday for a Street Child DVD with all you need to put on a really inspirational presentation about the work that God is doing through Toybox with the street children of Latin America.

What's the point?

By sharing the stories of these extraordinary children you can be part of bringing hope to their lives. Your church and its members can do this is a number of ways but the very best way is to join the Child Ambassador Scheme – and full details of this scheme and sign-up forms for distribution in your church are included on the DVD.

One + One = changed lives

To bring about change in the lives of street children in Latin America we want to set your church the challenge of finding:
- 1 x Child Ambassador Scheme supporter
- 1 x commitment to pray

Act today Simply sign up online to receive your pack or call 0845 466 0010 or email info@toybox.org and ask for a 'Toybox Sunday for a Street Child DVD'

www.toybox.org.uk

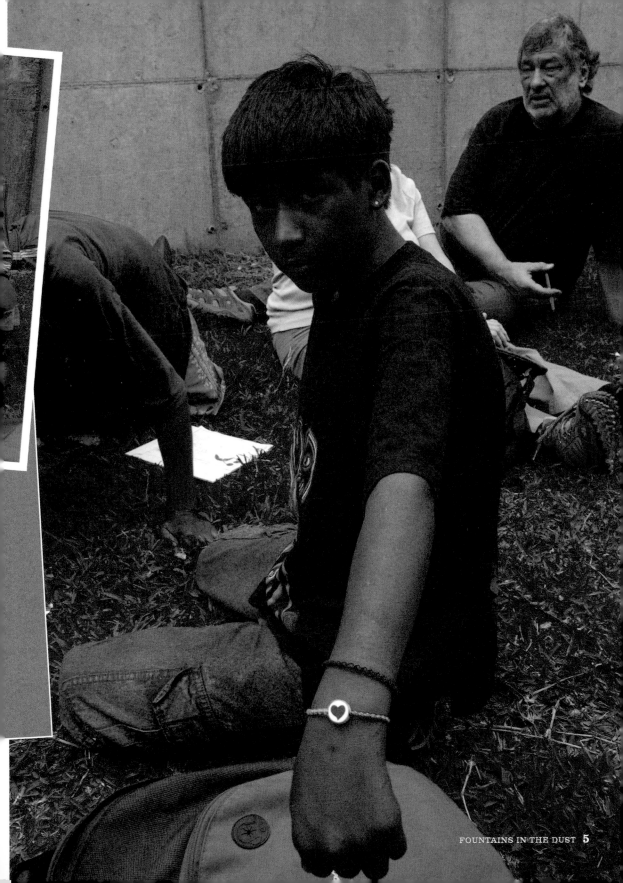

Martin

There used to be a programme called *Zoo Quest* on the television years ago. I loved watching it. David Attenborough, one of my personal heroes, would travel to some exotic location on the other side of the world, hunting for scarce and sometimes very bizarre animals that had rarely been filmed, let alone captured. A local guide was essential to all of these adventures; someone who knew the local terrain and could offer essential advice in the pursuit (and avoidance) of creatures that might be dangerous to human beings.

I remembered that series as we set out to meet homeless street kids in Peru for the first time. As far as Bridget and I were concerned, everything was new and unknown. We had just arrived in Latin America. Never been there before. We had no idea what to fear, what to expect or what to hope for. We felt nervous and jittery. Would we be risking physical danger in our quest to spend time with these children who lived out their strange, independent lives in the shadows of Lima? And how would they react to us? Why on earth should they be expected to tolerate the stares and foolish questions of people who had nothing concrete to offer them? No point in us blithering on about going back to the United Kingdom to raise awareness and funding. It would mean nothing.

Our guide was a man called Martin (pronounced 'Marteen'), a slight but wiry individual with penetrating dark eyes and an air of watchful confidence.

He carried a rucksack, but with the flap tied down so that Bridget and I, nosey as ever, were unable to see what was in it. Apparently Martin was a Street Educator, whatever that might turn out to mean, and he was attached to a children's home somewhere in the city. That was all we knew. When every piece of dialogue involves interpretation it is not easy to ask all the questions that spring to mind.

Tension mounted as we approached an exceptionally wide street in a part of the city where, according to Martin, street children were likely to be found. He would go on ahead, he explained through our interpreter, and we could follow when the time was right. Eventually we were asked to cross one half of the street and wait by a railing in the middle of a broad central

reservation. Here a steep slope dipped sharply down onto a sort of wide grassy runway that stretched for two or three hundred yards away from us, running parallel with the main road.

In the distance, about a hundred yards away, we could see Martin sitting cross-legged on the grass. He was not alone. Other figures knelt or sat around him in a rough semicircle. One or two were stretched out on the short-cropped turf. Against the base of the walls that lined the grassy strip we could see what looked like elongated heaps of cloth or newspaper. More people, perhaps? Sleeping children? The scene reminded me of something. A few seconds later, I realized what it was.

Prayers are answered In strange ways, aren't they? Ever since I exchanged one set of problems for another by becoming a Christian back in the mid-sixties, there has been a little dream or yearning inside me. I have always wanted to know how it would have looked and felt to be with Jesus. What kind of ethos or atmosphere surrounded his encounters with people who discovered that, amazingly, the man who did the miracles, the one who called himself Son of Man and Son of God, the one who in some mysterious way was God himself, wanted to be with them and actually managed to make them feel better about themselves?

> Against the walls that lined the grassy strip we could see what looked like elongated heaps of cloth or newspaper. Sleeping children?

It looked so quiet. So relaxed. So spectacularly ordinary.

FOUNTAINS IN THE DUST

Gazing down at Martin and the tableau of figures surrounding him, I knew, with the unquestioning certainty that we sometimes experience in dreams, that it must have been very much like this. It looked so quiet. So relaxed. So spectacularly ordinary. Not for the first time, I asked myself why we are continually bamboozled into seeking solutions in the rushing winds, the shattering earthquakes and the raging fires of human struggle and striving, when the answers lie, as they always did, in the still small voice of love. Love does all the little, crucial things consistently and untiringly. It builds a dwelling place for trust and safety that is much less likely to fall because the foundations have been painstakingly laid.

And when we were finally allowed to make our perilous way down the slippery slope to join Martin and the children, what kind of sophisticated ploys and programmes were being used with these unloved, unwashed pilgrims who had already seen far too much of the dark jagged night in their short journey through life? The answer is that they were making friendship bracelets and colouring in pictures on the printed sheets that Martin had brought along in that precious rucksack of his. Whatever else they may have seen or been or done, these were boys, and boys, to adapt a phrase, will always default to being boys. Heads bent, brows knitted, tongues protruding from the corners of their mouths, they concentrated hard on the things they were doing and were proud of the results. But there was much more going on than that.

There is a verse in the twenty-ninth chapter of the book of Job in the Old Testament, in which Job is looking back to the good old pre-boil days when, as a representative of God, he regularly addressed the people.

'When I smiled at them,' he recalls, 'they could scarcely believe it.'

That was what was going on with Martin and these lads. And the smile they received was not just an expression on his face. It was a nod of approval, a serious focus of interest on something that was said or done, the slightest touch of his hand on a shoulder or an arm, an aura of affection that bathed an ordinary conversation in unaccustomed light. He knew many of them well from repeated encounters in the past, but still, one sensed, they could scarcely believe it. For reasons that were not accessible to their understanding, someone was smiling at them. They were liked. They were respected. They were valued.

So there we are. That is what a Street Educator does. At any rate, that is what Martin does. As he gets to know individuals he encourages them to think about entering a project where meals and clothes and care and education will be provided, but sadly the equation is not as simple as it may

there are grown-ups who care about them without wanting or expecting anything in return

appear. The street may be bleak and dangerous, but community takes many different forms. For so many of these children safety lies in places and faces and patterns that are as reassuringly familiar as they are harsh.

Whether or not they opt for life in one of the available projects, these boys receive something of inestimable value from people like Martin. They receive the surprising good news that there are grown-ups who care about them without wanting or expecting anything in return. Against all the heavily stacked odds, there is such a thing as unconditional love and, whether they realize it or not, that kind of love can come from only one source. They have encountered the Good News of Jesus.

One by one they appeared, stumbling and yawning from their sleeping holes under the graffiti-covered bridge

Teenagers

We had come to the bridge over the River Rimac and at first it appeared that our attempt to make contact with some older street children was in vain. We stood there, the six of us and Martin, as buses rattled past, petrol fumes and dust filling our lungs, feeling dislocated and weary. What now?

'Just wait,' said Dennis, quietly.

And sure enough, as we waited, one by one they appeared. They made me think of rats seeking out the Pied Piper; scrambling up the bank from where they had been scavenging in the litter-strewn mud of the river bank; stumbling and yawning from their sleeping holes under the graffiti-covered bridge; emerging as if by magic from the crowded nearby streets.

I think my first overall impression was of a group of misshapen, wizened, little old men who appeared to be dressed bizarrely in vastly oversized teenage gear. They seemed to have lost a lot of teeth and, because their cheeks had sunk, those teeth that remained were protruding as well as being yellow and chipped. They looked so neglected and poorly that I found myself remembering something Dennis had told us only that morning. Life expectancy for street kids is generally estimated to be only four years after they take up life on the streets, so most of these lads may indeed be advanced in years. Apart from alcoholism and drug addiction, many of them suffer from skin funguses, malnutrition and respiratory illnesses so advanced that when they finally make it to a hospital, usually carried by their mates, it often turns out to be their first and last visit.

The short time we spent with this group proved a surprise in so many ways. Martin had warned us to expect very little from the encounter, explaining that while the younger boys we had met in the morning still had a childlike appetite for life, by the time they reached their teens their bodies and minds were so ravaged by their lifestyle that they were pretty well unreachable. Sure enough, having greeted Martin with genuine pleasure, they formed a line and eyed us with open suspicion. Gringos (foreigners) have done nothing for them in the past, apart from providing them with a means of staying alive via access to their mobile phones and wallets. They stared openly and indifferently at us. We tried hard not to stare back and searched for a means to communicate.

'Do you know any English football teams?'

I watched their faces as Carys translated Adrian's question. They looked understandably puzzled by what must have seemed a random question but, even while keeping up their show of shrugging indifference, they were eager to demonstrate their knowledge. They were teenage boys, after all.

Chelsea was naturally their favourite because the Peruvian star Claudio Pizarro plays for them, but there were several who also referred to a quite different football team.

'Ah,' said Adrian, reaching into his bag.

> Life expectancy for street kids is generally estimated to be only four years after they take up life on the streets

My first impression was of a group of wizened little old men dressed in oversized teenage gear.

United by United?

 Why did I reach into my bag? I shall tell you. I wanted to pull out some items that proved as useful during our time in Peru and Bolivia as anything else we took with us. Let me explain.

Some years ago I mentioned in a book that my son Joe suffered from a serious but widespread neurosis. He was and is a fervent supporter of Manchester United football team. One morning a letter arrived with the familiar Manchester United logo printed at the top of the page. Manchester United writing to me? How exciting!

It turned out to be from a man called Keith Mackintosh, who is responsible for Health and Safety at Old Trafford. I had met Keith briefly some years earlier at a Christian event held in Manchester, but I had no idea that he was employed by the most famous football club in the world. Keith mentioned that he had read about Joe's lifelong attachment to United, and wondered if the two of us would be interested in coming up to see a match and have a look round behind the scenes.

'I realize,' he added, 'that you have a very busy schedule, but it would be nice if you could make it . . . '

Guess who hastily rearranged his very busy schedule.

Since that first trip Joe and I had enjoyed a number of excursions to the north-west, and my relationship with Keith had deepened into real friendship. When Bridget and I were in the middle of planning our trip to Latin America it occurred to us that something connected with Manchester United might be useful to show the children we were going to meet. So I contacted Keith.

Keith Mackintosh is the kind of man who never lets you down. Almost by return of post he sent us a package containing wads of team photos with signatures printed on the back and a collection of lapel pins decorated with the colourful Manchester United shield.

Did these things go down well with the boys we met on the streets and in the projects? I am happy to record that they did. It was quite amazing. Forget food, drink, the Bible or any other form of useful, inspiring or improving literature. Those soccer-related bits and pieces, and particularly the photos, were pored over with studied, consuming interest by every group of boys that we encountered. This older group of lads that Bridget mentioned, for instance, were almost instantly mellowed and disarmed by the discovery that we appeared to live on the same footballing planet as them. We already had some things in common, such trivia as humanity, latent spiritual awareness, a need for loving affirmation and the desire to build a positive future, but there was no doubt about the strongest bond of all. We were united by United. Thank you, Keith.

This older group of lads were almost instantly mellowed and disarmed by the discovery that we appeared to live on the same footballing planet as them

The Ice Lolly Challenge

Manchester United pictures had gone a long way towards breaking down a natural barrier. So did something which occurred shortly afterwards, and which required more courage from us than anything else that day.

Being handed a blue ice-lolly-style drink with the expectation that one should take a sip through the straw and pass it on is hardly an Indiana Jones moment, you might think. But when you have had it drummed into you that you should only clean your teeth in bottled water, only drink bottled water, only eat salad or fruit washed in bottled water and on no account buy ice cream or drinks from a street vendor you can see why a neon tongue-dyeing confection from a nearby street stall could prove worrying. Make no mistake, I was afraid. I was very afraid! Add to this the fact that the straw has already been sucked by a teenager with impetigo sores around his mouth and maybe you can begin to sense my dilemma. And it was not mine alone.

Smilingly putting the straw to my lips I glanced around our group to see six faces determinedly signalling their gratitude and pleasure at the prospect of sharing in this treat. We may have been worried, but we were of one mind. We had all witnessed Martin encouraging this group of lads to each put in a few *soles* in order to buy drinks to share with us. To show disrespect by refusing their generosity was out of the question.

Maybe the colossal amount of sugar killed off any bugs, maybe it was a miracle, anyway, none of us got ill. Even if we had, though, I think it would have been worth it. As we passed the drink round the circle two of the lads leaning on the rail of the bridge took cheap bundles of bamboo pipes out of their trouser pockets and coaxed tune after tune out of them. The sight of those stunted teenage football fans who had such little hope for the future, but who were entertaining us so cheerfully, saddened us all terribly and I think we were secretly relieved to say goodbye and slowly make our way back to the van. By the time we reached it and turned back to wave, they had vanished.

Section Two
Working Children

BOLIVIA & PERU

BRIEFINGS:
Working
Children

Whilst some of the working children on the streets of South America are street-living children, there are many more who have homes to go to.

They spend their days on the streets trying to earn money to help support their families.

The jobs they do include shoe-shining, cleaning cars, busking, begging, selling sweets on buses and working in the mines. Many are employed as 'yellers', whose job is to lean out of bus windows and loudly advertise their destinations to passers-by, in order to attract custom.

Some working children tell us that their parents don't allow them home until they have earned the required amount of money each day.

Whilst some working children are able to go to school, many are not.

A Working Child

 She is so small. Her filthy hair is dragged into matted twists, her cheeks are bruised by the wind and roughened by ingrained dirt, her lightless eyes are dulled from neglect, mucus from her runny nose drips unattended onto her baby lips.

In her maybe three years of being in this world she has probably never been cuddled. Never had a bubbly bath, never had her hair piled on top of her little head in fun baby shampoo shapes. Never had a bedtime kiss.

She is so tired. She leans her little body wearily on the doorframe of the restaurant where we and the ambassadors have been eating lunch, and gazes emotionlessly at us as we laughingly crowd through the exit door. In response to her grandmother's terse command she hauls herself upright, stretches out her tiny arms to offer her handful of sweets and chewing gum for sale and tries to smile winningly at us. Not a glimmer of light brightens her deadened eyes, even when Ines crouches down to talk gently and lovingly to her. She has no hopes, no dreams, and no expectations that anything can be different. An abrupt word of command, and, with hard fingers digging into her shoulders, she is forcibly propelled forward and away from the danger of Ines' concern. Then she is gone, presumably to smile winningly elsewhere. She is a financial asset. She is a working child of Oruro. She is so very small.

She has no hopes, no dreams, and no expectations that anything can be different.

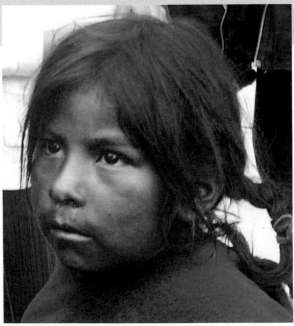

The Future President of Bolivia

When I first met Richard I have to admit that I didn't instantly consider him as a future presidential candidate. In many ways he simply seemed a fairly ordinary eleven-year-old lad. But the more I've got to know about him, the more I've realized that behind his smile and outward appearance lives a tenacious and deeply caring spirit.

Richard lives with his mum, dad, two brothers and five sisters in a very humble, one-room dwelling on the outskirts of the city of Cochabamba, in Bolivia. His dad is incredibly hard-working, and puts in as many hours as he can bricklaying in the local area. His mum is equally keen to provide for her family, but ill health prevents her from working as much as she'd like. In spite of their best efforts, the joint income is barely enough to provide for the children's needs. They are just about able to scrape together enough *Bolivianos* to meet the rental charges for their small room and to pay for regular water. Providing food and clothing on top of that is a huge, ongoing challenge.

That's where Richard comes in. Along with some of his brothers, Richard works at a bus stop, cleaning buses. The pay isn't great and the conditions are hardly ideal but Richard knows that every contribution really is vital.

I don't know how ambitious I would be if I were living in the conditions Richard has to call home. I'm also not sure how high my self-worth would be as I compared myself to the shoppers getting on and off the buses I cleaned. Would I look at them and wish my life was like theirs? Would their apparent wealth cause me to feel despondent, or would it spark dreams for the future in my mind and imagination?

As Richard has grown up in his eleven short years, he has begun to allow himself to dream. Encountering society through his work on the streets, he's begun to wonder if maybe, just maybe, he could somehow make a better life for himself and for others. And so, Richard hasn't just washed buses to help buy food for his family. Richard has washed extra buses, and has volunteered for any and every job because he is determined to get an education.

And amazingly, that's exactly what's happening. Richard still cleans buses, he still helps to provide for his family, but he has also saved enough money to help pay for the things he needs to go to school. His teachers say he's doing well. They describe him as a very caring boy, a natural leader, a responsible member of his class.

And so, for now at least, that's Richard's life. I wish he didn't have to clean so many buses. I wish he could have more free time just to play. I wish he didn't have to be so responsible. But I'm so thankful that, despite the circumstances of his life, Richard is making the best of it all. He's secure in his family and he's making a way through the world as best he can.

We asked Richard what he'd like to do in the future. His answer? He'd like to be the president of Bolivia. Failing that, he'd settle for being a lawyer. Richard's thinking isn't restricted by his present circumstances. He's able to see way beyond the difficulties of today. What a lesson for us all.

Hector is in charge of about fifty goats, on his own in the hills.

The Shoe-Shiners

I got on well with the shoe-shiners. There were four of them gathered in a little park in the central square of Oruro. One was a man, muffled up and suspicious of our intentions. He sat apart, a thin, troubled presence, and said very little. The other three were lads of fourteen or fifteen, warmly dressed against the challenge of chilly winds and cold nights, but happy to speak and be spoken to.

Jonny, the chattiest of the three, talked about life on the street. All three of them, he explained, had parents and homes some distance away from Oruro, but the boys had no choice other than to be financially independent. Without their small industry, and the essential collection of tools they lugged around constantly with them in wooden boxes, they would have no income at all. At the same time, they seemed determined that the future would bring something better. All of the boys talked about school, which they attended whenever possible, naming their favourite subjects and expressing a wish that they could be involved in full-time education.

Jonny talked with some passion about the situation in Bolivia: the need for the government to look after people properly and especially to help the many children who are born into poverty and hardship.

Once again the magical Manchester United pictures were received with wonder and satisfaction. A brisk chatter broke out as the three boys pointed

the boys had no choice other than to be financially independent.

Once again the magical Manchester United pictures were received with wonder and satisfaction.

out players that they recognized to each other, and tried to match them with signatures on the back of the sheets. For those few minutes they could have been teenagers in any environment, in any culture, in any part of the world.

It may seem a very small cause for elation, but, as our meeting came to an end, my friend Jonny found that his Man U poster fitted with millimetric precision into the lid of his shoe-shine box. Why did he and I find this so satisfying? Perhaps because life, whether in Bolivia or the United Kingdom, really is one great big jigsaw puzzle, and when you find even a tiny little piece that fits perfectly – well, there's always a chance that you might find another.

God bless Jonny and the shoe-shiners.

In the Early Hours

 I quietly drew back a sliver of curtain, just enough to be able to see into the street below. The rowdy dawn chorus of banging and shouting that heralded each market day in the centre of Oruro had barely begun, and Adrian was still sleeping. It was 5:30 a.m., grey, cold and raining so hard I could scarcely make out the entrance to the covered area of the market on the other side of the road. A slight movement caused me to peer more intently. Huddled together on a thin grimy blanket which offered no protection from the driving rain above or the wet paving stones beneath, were 'my' mother, daughter and baby girl.

For two days I had been watching them whenever we returned to our hotel. They made such a hopeless little picture. The mother seemed to be constantly trying to stop her small baby crying by alternately feeding and rocking her. The baby, her face almost hidden by a red woollen hat pulled down over her eyes, was huddled against her mother for protection. The older girl's tired little frame seemed to be permanently propped up listlessly against the entrance door, moving only to occasionally hitch a dirty blanket more tightly round her shoulders or pull her soggy straw hat over her eyes in a futile attempt to withstand the weather. Her legs were filthy from the mud and rain, her feet soaking and presumably cold in plastic flip-flops, her gloveless hands appearing permanently moulded into a begging bowl shape. I reflected that I had not seen her receive a single coin during the periods I watched her, but I supposed she must have been given something, otherwise why would they be taking up their positions again so early in the morning?

It was all just too awful, and I let go of the curtain and returned to my bed. But I couldn't sleep, and as soon as Adrian was up and awake I begged him, in the few minutes we had before we were picked up to visit our planned projects, to let us take something, anything, over to this little family. We had hardly any *Bolivianos*, but we had some fruit and biscuits left from a welcome basket given to us by our hosts, so we slipped across the road and decanted what we had into the cold, wet hands of the standing girl and the lap of the seated woman. To be honest I anticipated no response except for a slight easing of my own guilt, but the tableau sprang into life. Clasping both Adrian's hands in hers, the mother thanked him with tears streaking her face while amazed joy quite simply transfigured the face of the little girl who, at close quarters, turned out to be about eight years old. She gazed incredulously backwards and forwards from the rosy red apple in her cupped hands to me. She almost skipped in her excitement. Her smile illuminated the dreary street, her eyes huge shiny pools of gratitude!

The arrival of our bus abruptly terminated this encounter. We were never to see them again, and one blurry photo is all I have to remember them by. But we had witnessed the small miracle once more.

We give rags. They receive riches.

One blurry photo is all I have to remember them by.

Section Three
Horrors of
San Sebastian Square

Cochabamba is the third largest city in Bolivia.

It is home to the world's largest statue of Christ, at 33 metres or 109 feet tall.

Situated on San Pedro hill, the statue provides visitors with a panoramic view of the city.

An internal staircase allows tourists to climb up inside and provides access to the highest viewing points.

Despite being one of Bolivia's most economically and socially progressive cities, Cochabamba is also home to hundreds of Bolivia's 2,500 street children.

Many of these children live together in self-made communities in places such as San Sebastian Square, one of the central park areas within the city.

COCHABAMBA, BOLIVIA

The Head Came in by Helicopter

The head came in by helicopter
Not the body
That came up in trucks
The body of the Christ was far too big
To haul up all at once
And they had to haul it up
To get the damn thing there
To build the white monstrosity
With Ayatollah eyes
And not a trace of kindness in its face
Nor any human warmth
In that symmetrical embrace
They had to built it on the summit
Visible, but coldly uninvolved
With all the messy stuff
That happens at the bottom of the hill
Nothing given, nothing sacrificed
We climbed a thousand steps inside the hollow statue
Spiralled up towards the helicoptered head
And found that we were noticing
A nasty smell of urine in the body of the Christ
Far, far below the dead thing on the hill
The risen Lord of all creation
Ten years old and reeling from the damage to his head
Cradled someone's filthy infant in his arms
And looking up for just an instant
From the Square of San Sebastian
Saw that figure shining on the hill
Shook his head in puzzlement
And gently stroked his baby's head, and said
'Who is that man?'

Adrian Plass

COCHABAMBA, BOLIVIA

Dead Men Walking

Obediently we leaned against the side of the van and awaited orders. The late afternoon sun was shafting through tall elegant trees, dappling shade over what seemed to be a pleasant grassy park area in the centre of San Sebastian Square. It also appeared to be a very popular picnic spot, judging from the number of folk we could glimpse still lying about soaking up the last of the sun's rays. The serene atmosphere seemed curiously at odds with the stern warnings we had all received before leaving the van.

'Jewellery and watches off. Bags to be preferably left in the van, or held close to the chest. No cameras. And above all, wait until you are told it is okay to leave the side of the van. Oh, and try and look as inconspicuous as possible.'

Adrian tried hard to look inconspicuous: not easy when you are a foot taller than almost everyone else. I tried to look nonchalant. Truth to tell, we were feeling a little bewildered.

We watched Julia cross the road and stop. She spoke into her mobile phone for a moment, and then replaced it in her pocket. She stood with her back to us peering from side to side. She seemed to be waiting for a signal – but what?

Suddenly, there appeared to be a slight disturbance around what from

a distance looked like a collection of broken cardboard boxes in the centre of the park. The atmosphere around the van became electric. Still no one spoke and I could see nothing to merit the change in dynamic. The only new arrival was a large middle-aged woman in a wheelchair, who was being methodically pushed across the square by a tall, emaciated younger man.

For want of something better to do, I watched the odd couple's arrival with interest. Her huge round glasses glinted in the sun, giving her face a moon-like quality, and she clutched an absurdly large leather handbag on her lap. Her ample, gathered skirts reached almost to her ankles, which were swollen and seemed misshapen. There was something faintly disturbing about her long, thick girlish plait and huge straw hat, which was jauntily adorned with lots

of large, brightly coloured plastic flowers and secured under her chin with thick elastic. Perhaps it was the contrast between her appearance and that of her tall unkempt carer, whose unusually long straggly hair poked out from under a scruffy black baseball cap. Or perhaps it was just my imagination.

Slowly they made their way down one of the concrete paths to the centre, and as they did so two things happened simultaneously.

The first was Daniel's face breaking into a huge smile as he whispered happily, 'It's okay, she's here.' The second was a strange tremor on the surface of the park. A whiffle of wind seemed to be stirring bits of cardboard, and sheets of old newspapers gently bowled over the grass. Then, almost as if they were in slow motion, living forms began to emerge, apparently from nowhere. From where we stood the effect was of zombies rising slowly from their tombs as, from all over the park, figures began a slow lurching march towards the wheelchair, accompanied by dogs that seemed incapable of walking more than two steps before collapsing in a stupor.

At that moment Julia came running towards us.

'Quickly, quickly, can you help us? Two rolls in each bag!' she said, excitedly, handing Adrian and I a pile of sandwich bags and pointing to a dustbin sack of ham and cheese rolls in the back of the van. Feverishly we stuffed bags, made fumble-fingered by the urgency in her voice, and shoved them unceremoniously into the large carrier bag she was holding out. Then we scurried after her into the park, aware that Matt and Dave were doing the same from the boot of their taxi, filling a cardboard box with their finished bags. I confess my initial bewilderment had turned to a degree of horror as we drew nearer to the rapidly increasing crowd, who by now had formed a heaving mob around the woman in the chair.

What sort of people were these? Every one of them appeared to be grotesquely disfigured in some way. Filthy hair, puffy eyes, dried blood on cut lips, purpling bruises, missing or blackened teeth, horrendous scarring; all made worse by the overpowering stink of glue from small plastic bottles stuffed into swollen misshapen nostrils. Tiny dirty children ran in and around the crowd, now bizarrely settling themselves into a rough semicircle around the woman in the chair.

'She's told them to sit down if they want food,' whispered Katya in my ear. 'She's explaining who we are and telling them we are here because we care about them. Now she's asking Carys to say grace and after that she says they can have the food.'

'But who is . . . ?'

I stopped abruptly. An extraordinary silence had fallen and, as Carys nervously prayed, I sensed relief at this moment of peace and order in the middle of their chaos. I opened my eyes to eager faces and felt relief that at least now I had something useful and straightforward to do. Smiling, I began to hand out my supplies but almost immediately realized that something was

I opened my eyes to eager faces
and felt relief that at least now
I had something useful and
straightforward to do.

going terribly wrong. The woman in front of me was practically snarling at me, waving her bag in my face and shouting something I didn't understand. Frantically, I turned to Katya.

'What's she saying?'

'That she hasn't got any chocolate milk. She wants it for her child.'

'But why on earth does she think I've got any chocolate milk?'

Tension was escalating rapidly and Daniel, realizing there was a problem, began grabbing back the sandwich bags we had just distributed with such confidence and picking up some of those which had been hurled to the ground in disgust. He bundled them into the discarded cardboard box and looked round.

'Bridget – quickly, quickly – come!'

As we set off running back to the van he hurriedly explained that Matt and Dave, arriving in the taxi, had been supplied with small sachets of chocolate milk to put into their bags, but we hadn't had any in our van. Hence the anger from those who felt they had been deprived.

'Two sachets to a bag. We must be quick.'

On our return the box was snatched out of our hands by a large and very aggressive man who nevertheless turned out to be actually trying to help. Certainly he did a lot of shouting at those who tried to jump the queue for the replenished bags of food, but the box was practically wrestled from his arms and torn apart as the crowd scrabbled for the remaining bags. Within minutes it was over. Even the remains of broken cardboard box had gone, trailed over the ground by a teenage boy who presumably saw it as a potential bedcover for the night ahead. I looked around. Everywhere folk were sitting on the grass munching away and chatting calmly to each other. Apart from one man so high on substances that he was eerily dancing round the group with his two ham rolls held up over his head like rabbit's ears, the atmosphere almost resembled that of a large family picnic. That's if you ignored the fact that they all seemed to have mastered the art of eating with one hand while holding a plastic gluepot to their nostril with the other. The fumes were overpowering, and I noticed several of the dogs, presumably woken by the scent of food, haul themselves to their feet and stagger a few yards before their legs gave way under them and they settled back into doped slumber.

But the atmosphere was far friendlier and, someone having given permission for Matt to take photos, there was quite a line-up to show off scars and share stories of atrocities suffered at the hands of other gangs and the police. I noticed that Adrian and Dave were filming an informal interview with a young man and his small child. Ange was sitting quietly on the ground with a little family group and had got stuck into a game of checkers. Carys was listening to a young woman who was carelessly breast-feeding her week-old baby, taking huge bites out of her ham roll and chatting animatedly while all the time inhaling glue; a new slant to the term 'multi-tasking'. My fleeting role as food distributor over, I felt very much a spare part and wished for the hundred and fiftieth time that I had made more effort to learn Spanish.

And then I saw him. About ten years old, he stood quietly holding a baby of around eight months in his arms. His eyes were blurred, one of them half closed by the puffiness, his lips grotesquely cut and swollen, his nose misshapen by the constant inhaling of toxic substances. But none of these sights were as shocking as the long untreated gash on his forehead, healing slowly into a disfiguring gaping hole. His clothes were filthy, his skin ingrained with dirt, his tattooed arms stick-thin. An aura of utter hopelessness, as potent as any stink of glue, enveloped him. He was a living picture of the reasons why hundreds and thousands of people all round the world feel the need to prevent children from taking to the streets. And what did I do? Unable to communicate verbally, angry, helpless and utterly useless, I couldn't bear to look at him any longer. I turned and walked away, myself a living picture of why so many hundreds and thousands of people all round the world turn their backs on these very same vulnerable, needy scraps of humanity . . .

Apart from one man so high on substances that he was eerily dancing round the group with his two ham rolls held up over his head like rabbit's ears, the atmosphere almost resembled that of a large family picnic.

It's Not the Winning, It's the Taking Part that Counts

I sat opposite my opponent, ready to begin our game of checkers. Until that moment it hadn't been the most conventional of ways to approach a game. The young person sitting across the board from me was, as far as I could tell, living on the streets. He looked somewhere in the region of sixteen or seventeen years of age. He was sitting in the midst of many others who also called the streets their home. There were young children, street families, older men, older ladies. A whole cross section of people with one thing in common: they had nowhere to live, and had congregated together, perhaps for safety, perhaps for community, perhaps by chance.

For some reason, this young man's face jumped out at me from the crowd. It wasn't because he was louder than the others or more charismatic. It wasn't because he wanted to be noticed or because he was behaving oddly. It was because he was simply sitting there, in a crowd yet all by himself. Sometimes we can feel at our loneliest when we are surrounded by a vast number of other people. As I looked over towards this boy, I wondered if that was what his eyes were saying, 'I may appear connected but I'm actually all alone.'

As I wandered in his direction I noticed a box near him with the words 'Chess and Checkers' on the outside. I wasn't sure who it belonged to but, as I carefully and quietly sat down beside him, I tentatively suggested that he might like to join me in a game. I could tell from his eyes and the bags of glue and solvent lying all around that he'd been sniffing glue during the day. Solvent abuse can dramatically affect the way the children respond. It slows them down and takes them out of reality. However, even with a bit of compensation for the effects of the glue, I was aware that I was getting nothing at all back from him. No real acknowledgement that I was there. Not one word of communication. Nothing.

As my eyes surveyed his expressionless face, I could only imagine the pain and trauma his body had experienced during his relatively short time

on this earth. I'd worked with street children in the past and I knew it wasn't uncommon for them to choose not to speak. In many cases, the longer they have been on the streets, the harder it is to draw them out of themselves. I wondered how long he had been addicted to drugs. How many times had he been rejected? Was it possible that even the faintest spark of hope might still be found somewhere within his heart? I knew I could only guess at the stories and horrors that lay behind those eyes.

I was aware the odds were stacked against me with this lad, but I'm not generally one to give up easily. My friends tell me I can be a little bit stubborn. I prefer to say I'm tenacious! And this was one of those occasions when I was determined to keep going: to try to engage; to attempt to communicate; to try to share something positive with this young lad. And so, as he hadn't actually verbally declined my offer of a game, I decided to open the packet, set up a game of checkers and see what happened. I was amazed to find that once the game was out he was more than happy to join in. He still didn't speak, but nonetheless he was playing.

I decided from the outset that it would be best not to try too hard. Now that I'd got this lad to participate, I felt it would be highly inappropriate to

He didn't say yes but he didn't say no either.

thrash him in game one. Besides which, I wasn't even sure that he would know and understand the rules. However, a few minutes in and I was confident he knew exactly what he was doing. He still didn't speak. He didn't really show any emotion. But he concentrated carefully before making his moves. And he won game one.

Congratulating myself on my success at both engaging this lad in a game and letting him win, I decided to try again and gently suggested we have a re-match. He didn't say yes but he didn't say no either. So I reset the board and he dutifully joined in, allowing me to make the first move on this occasion. Obviously, with our developing checkers relationship now in full flow, I felt it would be okay to start trying now. He'd won game one so it would surely be fine for me to win game two.

So, with my strategic checkers brain fully engaged, match two began. And finished. Fairly quickly. And I lost. It surprised me, as I like to think I'm quite good at strategic games!

Within minutes, we had game three set up and ready to go. By this point, a young boy of around five or six had wandered over to see what was happening. Despite his surroundings and environment, this young child still had something of a spark in his eyes. He was less distrustful than his older companions, and still brave enough to explore and engage. He quickly realized I was in need of a bit of help and decided we should become a team. And so game three began, as junior and I set about beating the reigning champion. And we lost.

By this point, the street workers we were with had decided it was time for us to leave so I tidied up the checkers counters, shook hands with my opponent, thanked him for the game and prepared to leave. I never found out his name. He never really communicated with me verbally. He didn't outwardly show any sign of emotion, positive or negative. But maybe, just for a moment at least, he felt a little bit of acceptance. I expect I'll never know and I'll probably never see him again, but I'm glad we could share that short time together. Even if he was much better than me at checkers!

Some of my travelling companions found it amusing that I was well and truly thrashed by a lad on the streets who was so clearly under the influence of a significant amount of solvent. But you know, sometimes that saying is true – it's not the winning, it's the taking part that counts.

Ange's Back

 I remember noticing Ange's back while she sat and played checkers in San Sebastian Square. My own mind was full of tumult as I tried to absorb and understand some of the dreadful sights before me, and, by contrast, her back was so very, very still. She appeared to be giving her whole attention to this small activity, as though the game of checkers she was playing on this particular day in this particular place was the most important thing in the world. In a way, it was. This tiny little capsule of contact between two people would never happen again. It was unique, and therefore might as well be perfect. I am beginning to realize how essential it is to give myself and my attention unreservedly to people and situations that are in front of me *now*. The memory of Ange's back will help.

They Call Her Mum

Hurting and confused and thoroughly out of sorts with myself, I wandered over to where the woman in the wheelchair was parked. The flowers on her hat bobbed and danced as she laughed and chattered with a crowd of young people, who were relaxing in a semicircle in front of her, their faces transfigured with something that looked very much like love.

'They call her mum, you know,' said Daniel, quietly appearing at my elbow.

'But who is . . . ?' My question hung in the air again as Daniel ushered me forward and introduced me. Bending down to her level I found myself looking into eyes that sparkled with humour and acceptance, and I saw that she was beautiful. Clearly she longed to speak to me as much as I did her, but our communication was mostly with our eyes as Daniel did his best to translate our conversation.

'Someone from England – how wonderful.'

'It's wonderful to be here with you.'

'No, no, you are the ones who are wonderful to come.'

'It's a privilege to meet you.'

'No, it is I who am privileged to meet you.'

Admittedly Daniel's translating skills were limited, but there was no doubt our conversation lacked a bit of originality. It didn't really matter. I was in the presence of one of God's angels and I knew it. Calling Carys over, I was able to find out a little more.

Her name was Ana Maria. Yes, it was true they called her mum: 'Mama Anita'. Anita means little Ana – 'much more affectionate than just Ana.'

Yes, God had called her many years ago to work with the street people. 'Well, what happened was that God had put these people into my heart and they just wouldn't get out!'

She went on to tell us that street children in Bolivia are treated worse than animals, especially by the police who beat the children and force them to give them what they have stolen. She comes to the streets several times a week bringing soup which she has made from ingredients she has bought from the market.

'Giving out food is a way of making contact with the children. I encourage them to come to one of my homes.'

She runs two homes, one of which is especially for girls because it is so important to keep them safe from harm. She wishes we had time to come and meet her girls. She is planning to build another home with some prize money she won two years ago. No, she doesn't mind having her photo taken and will even take her hat off for the occasion. Please, please will we try and come again one day? Her people need so much to know someone cares.

We hug, we kiss, we look into each other's eyes and I recognize a soulmate. And I know I could never in a million years do what she is doing.

'So, come on Daniel, who is she?' Trundling back to the office in the van, I was finally able to ask my question.

'Well, I don't know so very much,' Daniel looked rueful. 'I know she contracted polio when she was two and has been in a wheelchair ever since. I know that Pepe, her assistant, was once a drug addict who she rescued from the streets. He adores her – goes everywhere with her. He

'Well, what happened was that God had put these people into my heart and they just wouldn't get out!'

calls himself her secretary. I know when she was about twelve God called her and told her he could use her despite her paralysis. And I know she is a lovely lady with a huge heart who has been helping street people for many, many years. Oh, and now she is a spy for us.'

'She's a what?'

'A spy, for us at Early Encounter Project. She keeps an eye out for any new children she sees on the streets and lets us know. She also tries to encourage them to seek help before they get sucked into street life. And she helps us with first contact, as you saw this afternoon. We would not have felt safe to go in among those people without her.'

'And her prize?'

Clearly Ana Maria hadn't made a lot of this as no one seemed to know the answer, and the subject was temporarily shelved.

That evening, back at our hotel at last, we must have presented a somewhat crushed group. We were all pretty shell-shocked by the day. The hope and positive energy from a day spent with children gathered together from many projects had been followed by such horrific glimpses of degradation in San Sebastian Square. All of us except Angela, who had seen it all before, admitted to having felt quite scared and de-skilled by the experience.

Adrian and I talked about our encounters with poverty elsewhere in the world. Slums in Bangladesh. Townships in South Africa. Villages raddled with AIDS in Zambia. These were communities joined by poverty and potentially defeating circumstances, but in every case we had seen the human spirit fighting to overcome, displaying a dignity out of all proportion to the problems faced. But here, in the comparatively pleasant surroundings of Cochabamba, we had witnessed what happens when folk fall so deeply into the gutter of life that it is easier to stay down there in the slime than risk attempting the long climb out, only to be hurled back yet again. We had seen the women displaying their stomach scars – evidence of self-harming, heard the stories of frequent violent attacks, and witnessed the effects of addiction, the evidence of stealing and the shamelessness of the open glue-sniffing. Our spirits were very low as we discussed the probable future of the little children and especially the newborn baby we had seen. We drifted off to bed early.

One sentence I had heard that afternoon was still ringing in my ears as I tried to get to sleep that night. 'They call her mum.' In the middle of that apparently impenetrable darkness one small light was shining very strongly indeed – a light called Ana Maria.

I found myself looking into eyes that sparkled with humour and acceptance

In the middle
of that
apparently
impenetrable
darkness one
small light
was shining
very strongly
indeed – a
light called
Ana Maria.

The internet was notoriously unreliable in the hotel where we were staying. It wasn't until we returned home that I was able to access anything that might tell me a bit more about the extraordinary woman I had met that afternoon and her 'prize'. At last, hidden among information regarding various awards given for service to children, I found her.

Her full name turned out to be Ana María Marañon de Bohorquez, and she has actually been helping addicts and street children in Cochabamba for over thirty years. Single-handed, and despite her disability, she has set up two homes, 'The Children's Rescue Ark' and 'Rose of Sharon', trying to provide the children she rescues from the streets with security, love and hope for a future. Every week she visits the streets to show she cares for her 'children', whatever their age and however far down they have sunk. And two years ago this extraordinary selfless work was internationally recognized. She was selected by the World's Children's Prize for the Rights of the Child, sharing the platform in Sweden with no less than Nelson Mandela and winning the World's Children's Honorary award for 2005. With the prize money she has bought land in preparation for building yet another home.

So, quite a megawatt lighthouse-style beam actually!

Asking 'Why?'

It's not just three-year-olds who have a tendency to keep asking 'why?'. I do it too. Hopefully not in the repetitively irritating out-loud sort of way that toddlers might, but it happens all the same: in my mind; in my heart; in my spirit.

The tendency to ask why can be a good thing. Asking why can lead to new discoveries. It's the sign of an inquisitive mind, one that wants to understand and to challenge. But there are times when asking why just doesn't work. As hard as I try, there are questions in this life to which I'll never get a satisfactory answer. No matter how many times I ask them.

I caught myself asking why a lot on one particular evening in Cochabamba, Bolivia. We'd come to meet the street children of San Sebastian Square. Whenever you arrive in a new place, full of new encounters and new faces, it can take a while to get your bearings. This night was no different but as my eyes scanned the world before me it wasn't long before I noticed a tiny baby amongst the group. I think this small new life caught my attention because it looked so out of place.

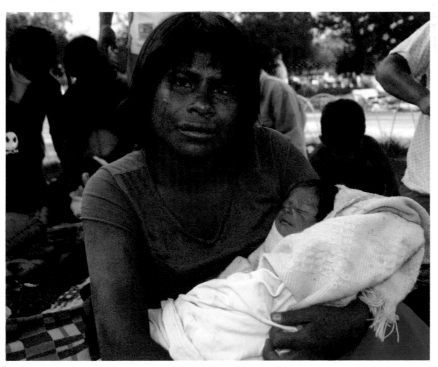

Newborn babies aren't meant to be living here. Where was the freshly-painted nursery, the cuddly toys, the mobile over the cot, the New Baby cards, the box of nappies, the pile of babygros and the constant stream of visitors? None of those things for this little child.

The warmth and security of home had been replaced by the harsh reality of street life. No first images of smiling faces for this baby, just scenes of glue-sniffing and alcohol. And it wasn't just the sights, but the smell. The fumes from solvent abuse were almost overpowering for me. How much more so for this tiny baby, so perfectly formed, so at risk of being harmed?

The mother of the infant looked apprehensive as I tentatively sat down on the grass next to her. Pieces of cardboard and bottles of glue were strewn across the ground around us. Some people were chatting, others were sleeping, yet more were gazing vacantly across the park. I looked into her eyes and smiled, hoping to ease the tension. I can only imagine what was running through her mind. What was I doing there? Why did I want to engage with them? What did I want with her and her baby?

Street children survive against the odds. They are only too aware of the risks around them, which is undoubtedly why this young mum was looking at me with such suspicion. She must have learnt that adults are not to be trusted. She's learnt to protect herself from the dangers of the world and now she has the added challenge of protecting her baby too.

I tried to strike up some kind of conversation with her. To begin with I thought it was likely to go nowhere but she finally broke her silence and spoke a few words. She told me her baby was a boy. He'd been born seven days earlier. She hadn't named him yet. She finished by telling me

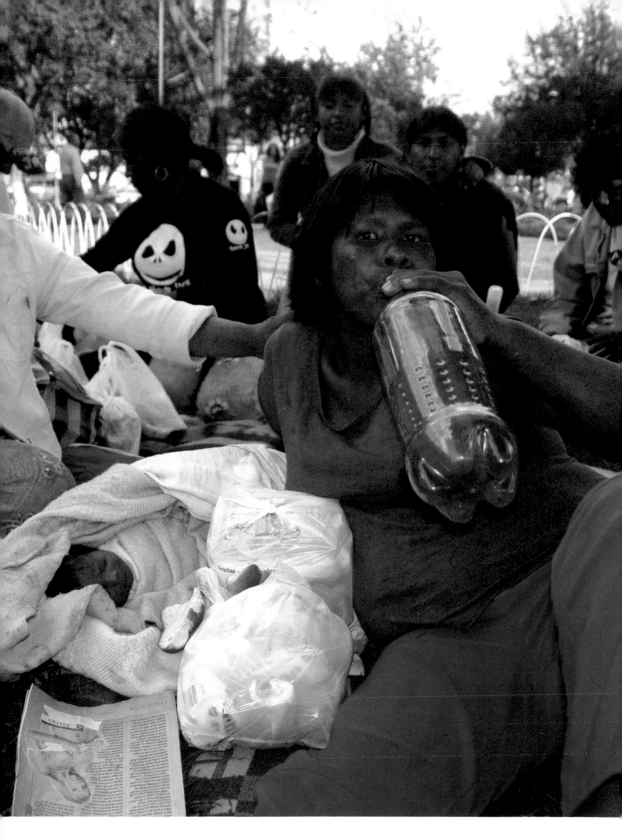

mother and baby were doing well. And that was clearly my cue to leave. I wasn't going to get any further with this new family – not today anyway.

As I went to bed in my hotel later that night, the words 'mother and baby are doing well' were of little comfort to me. No child should have to live on the streets. Every evening spent with the street kids confirms that within me even more. But I'm never more affected than when I encounter a brand new life; born on the streets and ever so likely to die on the streets too. It leaves me feeling powerless to help, frustrated with myself and with the world of which I am a part.

And so, as I lay in bed trying to make sense of things, I found myself asking why. Why is the world like this? Why is this baby boy living here, aged seven days, with no name, no home, and no hope for the future? Why does God allow this?

As I attempted to process these questions I began to realize that I was undoubtedly asking the wrong question. Instead of pouring so much energy into asking *why is it like this?* I needed to be asking *why can't it be different?*

I'm naturally inquisitive and I love to learn, so I never want to lose the wonder of asking why and discovering something new. But I also want to be the kind of person who asks the right 'why?' questions. I want to spend less time complaining about the mess, the darkness and the despair in the world and I want to spend a whole lot more time working out how I can bring light and hope into the world. If not for this particular baby, then for many others like him.

As I went to bed in my hotel later that night, the words 'mother and baby are doing well' were of little comfort to me. No child should have to live on the streets.

Section Four
The Joys of Travelling

Over the years the Plass family has managed to lose or nearly lose an astonishing variety of things, littering six continents with sunglasses, cameras, odd socks, cricket bats, essential documents, keys, books and one much-loved teddy bear called Gregory (don't worry, we got him posted back home from Sydney).

We have nearly lost

All our money to thieves in Spain

Half of Adrian's earlobe in New Zealand

Our daughter in Denmark

We have definitely lost

The will to live in Los Angeles airport

Most of every meal in Bolivia

Every bit of luggage on our first trip to Australia

Dignity in Peru

A few prejudices in Germany

Confidence in America

All our souvenirs to corrupt customs officers in Azerbaijan

Weight in Sweden and Switzerland (we couldn't afford to eat)

Our belief in marriage as an institution in quite a lot of places

And our hearts to thousands of children we have seen and met all over the world

But
We have never lost our passports! (At least, not yet . . .)

So far Ange has visited seventeen different countries, including Guatemala, which she has been to ten times with Toybox. While travelling she tends to find things rather than lose them, such as

Some fleas, while working with children on a rubbish dump in Guatemala City, which proved very hard to get rid of. She is pretty sure they've all gone now, though.

A rapid understanding of the fragility of life, when someone pointed a gun at her in a shanty town in Rio de Janeiro.

A deeper gratitude for the luxuries of running water, flushing toilets and dependable electricity when living in a children's home in Central America.

A parasitic infection in Guatemala. She'd like to remind everyone that when they advise you not to buy food from street stalls and to only clean your teeth in bottled water, they really mean it.

BRIEFINGS:
Lost and Found

Dreams

On the night before we left Peru to continue our journey to Bolivia my dreams were more vivid than usual. No doubt the change of diet, climate and environment had something to do with it. Beneath it all, perhaps, was the experiential shock of facing the same fact that had confronted us in our trips to Bangladesh and Zambia in the past. It is a very simple fact. There are millions of children all over the world who receive no support or care from anyone.

I know perfectly well that other people's dreams are about as interesting as someone else's winning rummy hand, but bear with me for a moment. The three dreams that I remember from that night are bizarre and absurd, to say the least.

The first one was a classic nightmare. Rivers of grotesquely small, vermin-like street children swarmed all over my legs and chest, biting viciously at my flesh with their little sharp teeth. I tried desperately to brush them off or slap them away from my body, but there were too many and they were too quick. I knew that I would soon be overwhelmed. It was terrifying.

The second dream was about my wife. For reasons that were not apparent, Bridget, who has never taken an illegal substance in her life, had become an addict. She was in a lost, pathetic state, and this time the dream was infused with deep, deep sadness rather than with fear.

The third dream, while far less dark and dramatic, was so utterly meaningless, so crazily irrelevant to any other element of my life that I hardly like to record it. Ah, well, here goes. In my third dream I was ceremoniously inducted as an honorary member of the Polish basketball team. Yes, that's right. The Polish basketball team.

A little scream of bewilderment rises in me as I consider this. Why Poland? I've never been to Poland. Why basketball? I played basketball once when I was twelve and have no interest in the sport. What on earth or in Poland would be the point of honorary membership of such an institution? I guess I just have to live in the mystery.

I was very glad to wake and get out of bed on the morning when we were to fly from Lima to La Paz. Nothing that we encountered in Bolivia was likely to be as frightening or as strange as the content of my dreams on that endless, thrashing night.

Nothing that we encountered in Bolivia was likely to be as frightening or as strange as the content of my dreams on that endless, thrashing night.

Hats . . .

The Aymara have existed in Bolivia and, to a lesser extent, in Peru, for over two thousand years and their traditional costume is still to be seen everywhere, especially among the women.

It consists of a below knee-length, softly pleated skirt called a *pollera*, which is traditionally made of fine materials such as velvet and brocade, but is more often made of all sorts of stuff. This is puffed out with underskirts to create a ballooning-hip effect that would be very unpopular in the UK. For festivals or important occasions women wear as many as five or six skirts on top of each other, so they appear extremely big-bottomed! When the winds are strong, warm knitted cardigans and sweaters are worn with brightly coloured shawls which are used to strap babies to their mothers' backs or to carry loads of goods. And the whole outfit is topped with either a straw hat decorated with vivid plastic flowers, or a bowler hat.

It was the bowler hats that most intrigued me. They appeared to be held on to the wearer's head by nothing more than gravity, so I set out to unravel the mystery, and in doing so discovered something very endearing about Bolivian people. They want to help to the point that they might make up anything just to keep you happy.

As a result of this I was told by an otherwise extremely intelligent and trustworthy guide that it was because the hats were so heavy that they did not fall off. How could I have swallowed the idea of cast-iron hats? But I did, until, that is, another person told me that when the women were young they took classes in hat retention, presumably like old-fashioned deportment lessons in which girls walked up and down flights of stairs with books balanced on their heads. Fell for that one too. Yet another normally sane individual told me that the women built their hair up high inside their hats. Marge Simpson style? Surely not! Over dinner one evening, determined to get to the bottom of this intriguing mystery, I asked one of our hosts to enlighten me.

'Oh, they keep them on with hat pins,' she replied, casually.

Of course they do! How silly of me!

I was told by an otherwise extremely intelligent and trustworthy guide that it was because the hats were so heavy that they did not fall off.

. . . And Dogs

Everywhere you go in Peru and Bolivia you meet dogs. They appear, trotting round the corners with a jaunty 'Can't stop, got to get on' air about them. They assemble in packs on street corners like teenagers with 'nuffin to do'. They disappear down alleys looking furtive. Sunbathe in parks. Hold up the traffic. Force you to step into the gutter.

And occasionally, just occasionally, you see them walking sheepishly along with adults, a resigned 'I suppose someone has to' droop to their shoulders.

Don't think I'll tell our dog, Lucy – she might get ideas.

The Day I Ate Half My Pizza

Ever since hearing about the Toybox projects in Bolivia I'd had a real desire to see them for myself. And so it was with great anticipation that I arrived in Bolivia, via the airport in La Paz. To say that my first night in Bolivia didn't quite live up to my expectations would be an understatement! Arriving in the middle of the night, we made our way directly to the hotel and went straight to bed. I was keen to get a good night's sleep as I knew we had yet another busy day ahead.

A few hours later and I realized that sleep was probably going to elude me for the rest of the night. Propped up against the wall in the bathroom, my body appeared to be fighting against itself and I knew it would be far too risky to move even a few metres away from the toilet. Everything seemed to hurt. Even breathing seemed to be a superhuman effort. Memories of a previous parasitic infection I'd picked up in Guatemala came flooding back to me. I racked my brains. I was sure I hadn't eaten anything I shouldn't. Had I?

Eventually, after what felt like one of the longest nights of my life, morning came and it was time for me to wander down to the hotel reception to make contact with a couple of the residents of La Paz for a prearranged meeting. I hadn't been out of my room for long when I realized I wasn't the only one feeling like this. Carys and Dave had experienced a similar night. And, as the hotel workers chatted to us, we realized we were simply suffering from altitude sickness – nothing more, nothing less. Not that this realization made the symptoms any more pleasant, but it did help my pride. I wasn't ill because I'd been careless and eaten the wrong thing. I wasn't ill because I was weak. I was ill because we'd flown to one of the world's highest airports, suddenly moving from sea level to more than 13,000 feet (over 4,000 metres). Surely anyone would be as ill as I was if they'd put their body through that.

Just as my feelings of weakness began to disappear, it happened. Adrian and Bridget appeared through the hotel door and said 'good morning'. It took a moment for me to register that they were there. I couldn't quite understand why they had entered through the front door. I had assumed they must be still tucked up in bed, feeling ill and reluctant to emerge into the day. However, not only were they already up and about, they had in fact had some breakfast, been for a walk and surveyed some of the local area! So much for being younger and fitter than them! On this occasion, they were proving themselves to be the most adaptable of us all.

A few hours later we were back at La Paz airport, preparing to fly on down to Cochabamba. Waiting around in airports often feels like a drag but on this occasion it felt as if we'd never be allowed onto the plane. I hate being ill. I especially hate being ill in foreign places. And I really hated having to use the stairs to get to the only set of toilets in the airport. Why, oh why, would you make passengers walk up and down stairs at such high altitude? Surely that must be bad planning.

three days
after we
arrived in
Bolivia, I
turned a
corner.

As you can see, my calm Christian exterior was attempting to hide a large range of emotions. I kept telling myself I was representing Toybox; I must not say the wrong thing. I was responsible for the group; I must attempt to stay in control. Inside I was a mess. I was angry at the airport. I was frustrated by the local people who all looked so healthy and could run and skip as if nothing was the matter. I was genuinely worried I could die as memories of an article I'd read on people dying from these symptoms floated back into my consciousness. My independent streak was being well and truly challenged!

Later that day we arrived in Cochabamba to be met by the local team. They were armed with small red and white pills. 'Take two of these,' they said to each of us, 'they'll make you feel better.' Usually I would never put unidentified drugs into my mouth but on this occasion, I felt I had nothing to lose and quickly swallowed the pills, hoping they would make me better rather than worse.

And, slowly but surely, I did get better. I'm not sure if it was the pills or just that I had started to adapt, but my body learnt how to function again and I began to feel that my time on earth was not about to come to an abrupt end. The days progressed as planned and I was able to participate fully, although I still found it difficult to contemplate eating much. But, three days after we arrived in Bolivia, I turned a corner. We went to a restaurant. I ordered a small vegetarian pizza. And I ate half of it. Doesn't sound much, does it? But trust me: it was a hugely important moment in my week. At last my body was accepting food. And at last I could reinstate my feelings of independence and control. That has to be a good thing, hasn't it?

Ridiculous Conversations

 I seem to specialize in ridiculous conversations, especially when I am in a foreign country. Here is an example.

We are about to start our lunch with a number of pastors and other guests. I decide to visit the lavatory first. I arrive to find that there is another man, a short stocky individual, waiting in the corridor for the toilet to become vacant. I lean against one wall; he leans against the opposite one. We look at each other and then hurriedly look away again. I suspect that we are thinking very similar things.

I am thinking, 'I ought to at least say *something* to this man, but given the fact that I speak no Spanish and he almost certainly speaks no English, the business of disentangling what we are saying to each other will have

only just begun when the toilet becomes vacant and we have to break off.' We continue to glance at each other occasionally in anguished silence. What on earth can the fortunate occupant of this toilet be doing that takes so long to accomplish? At last I can stand it no longer. I clear my throat and address the man in very slow English with, ludicrously, a slight Spanish accent. I try to sound bright and interested.

'Are you a . . . pastor?'

He looks at me in dismay, presumably aware that his answer could bring our conversation to an end before it has had a chance to begin.

'No.'

'Ah.'

I nod solemnly as though the man has said something of weighty significance. Another pause ensues. We both stare with fabricated interest at areas of paintwork and floor covering. Eventually, probably feeling that the onus is on him to continue our lively chat, he asks me exactly the same question.

'Are *you* a . . . pastor?'

Oh, God! I hunt in my mind for a reply that consists of more than one word, but fail miserably.

> I nod solemnly as though the man has said something of weighty significance.

'No.'

Now we both wish that we were dead. How long is this person going to take in the blessed toilet anyway? I have never seen anything as fascinating as the little piece of skirting board next to my left foot. After about three days my companion looks up, apparently inspired. He points at his own chest with his thumb, just in case I might suppose he is talking about someone else.

'I am a – children's worker!'

He smiles and nods vigorously, obviously feeling rather proud of this sudden wordy outburst. I must respond in kind. I also smile and nod as though all our little problems of communication have finally been solved.

'Ah! So, then, you work with – children.'

I watch the struggle in his eyes. Like me, he has run out of everything that would be required to extend this gripping piece of social intercourse. After this a great echoing void will open up and one or both of us will go completely mad.

'Yes,' he replies, wretchedly.

At this point the toilet door opens. Hallelujah! We are saved.

Section Five
Fountains in the Dust

BRIEFINGS:
Rescue – Life off the Streets

The teams Toybox supports in South America work to keep children with their families whenever they can.

When this is not possible, children need the love and care of a substitute family which, in the case of street children, is often found within small family-style children's homes.

The teams also encounter whole families on the streets. Keen to keep the family unit together, special rehabilitation projects have been developed to give whole families safety off the streets and to provide a stepping stone to a better future.

The Street in the Home

We are risking life and limb, standing in the middle of a street somewhere in the middle of Peru. Traffic thunders past us, the vehicles controlled by vociferous and extremely dangerous drivers. At the bottom of the street we can see a courtyard with a central circular stone seating area on which are perched several locals. Noisy informal ball games and table football are taking place in the courtyard which is lit by street lamps and surrounded by brightly painted buildings with attractive arched windows. The atmosphere is buzzing.

The only incongruous thing is the large stone archway at the top of the street into which is set a wooden door – which is shut. Oh, and the fact that the vehicles are battered small bicycles and scruffy skateboards, driven at ferocious speed by drivers who are mostly primary school age.

We are in Centro Shama, the extraordinarily inspirational concept of Frances Davinson who set out to find a way to successfully wean children off the streets, taking into consideration the fact that many have become almost feral through the survival techniques they have been forced to adopt, sometimes over many years.

Frances turns out to be a small homely woman whose gentle demeanour covers a hugely courageous and determined spirit and a brilliant mind. She is absolutely passionate about her innovative work here. Inviting us into the shelter and comparative calm of her small office, she tells us sadly that almost all of the children playing so confidently outside arrived in a desperately bad state.

'They are injured in their bodies and in their emotions. Do you believe that 90 per cent of these children have been raped?'

As we sit in shocked silence she goes on to explain that, for a few *soles*, a group of children can hire a tiny 'room': a concrete bunker to bed down in at night, all too well known to the many paedophiles who prey on their vulnerability. Most have also been physically abused by their parents, the police and even their teachers. They steal to eat, scavenge on the garbage dumps, live in packs and have minimal social skills, never having sat down to a meal or been disciplined in any way. Many have to be weaned off their addiction to *terocal* (glue) and alcohol. Hardly any can read or write. It is becoming a sickeningly familiar story, but in Frances we have met someone who has sought and discovered a solution.

Centro Shama is a street within a home. For many children the leap from street to a structured environment is a leap too far, causing them to run away, back to what they know. Frances, a trained engineer, has created a halfway environment: secure, loving and structured, but based on the children being able to exist for much of their day outdoors. Playing in the courtyard, curling up on street corners, seeking respite behind low brick walls, all these can take place with the additional blissful luxury that somebody cares and that at the end of the day they will go to sleep in their own bed without fear of molestation.

'And what they want most in their hearts,' continues Frances, 'is a family. They have experienced so much pain and abandonment that at first they cannot put their feelings into words, cannot bear to be touched, but time passes and they begin to trust, to establish relationships. They learn to be a child again. They can be restored.'

Of course it doesn't always work and Frances admits she is still recovering from the loss of a little boy who had been raped on so many occasions that he was unable to remember how many times it had happened. His spirit had been broken beyond recovery. He had run away only two months before our visit and no one had seen him since.

'I cried so much. I could not even pray. But I learnt many years ago that while my heart was bleeding I was not doing good for the other children, so now it affects me badly but I can carry on. I remind myself that I love the Lord. I love the Lord's call. And my children are the ones who stay here.'

And the marvellous truth is that for most of the thirty children living within these safe walls, the mixture of school, karate, singing and dancing, drama, painting, reading and writing, trips to the beach, free play and spiritual education, combined with professional counselling and lots of food is winning the battle.

We go back out into the sunshine to be grabbed by excited escorts, and led through another doorway into what seems to be their living room. Despite the comfy saggy sofas and rugs on the wooden floor there is a sense of healthy flexibility in this multi-purpose room. Sofas can be shoved to one side and rugs rolled up if there is fun to be had. With a great deal of ceremony and elaborate arm-gesturing we are ushered to a semicircle of green plastic chairs positioned in front of a huge television, and find ourselves watching a film made partly by a Peruvian television company and partly by Centro Shama.

Lying on rugs at our feet, leaning against our legs, some even snuggling up for a cuddle, are more than a dozen little boys. The film, based on the horrors of life on the streets, is graphic and upsetting, made more uncomfortable by the fact that we are watching it surrounded by the very children whose former lives it depicts. Do they recognize themselves? What effect does it have on them? Maybe we needn't worry. Cocooned now by the love and discipline of this exceptional home of healing, they are far more excited by the section showing them in their school uniforms, doing karate, eating their dinner and being recorded for the CD which they sell to raise funds for the home, than by any scenes of their former lives.

The finale of our visit is a high-energy live performance of their latest song, with jumps and shouts and dramatic sweeping arms and a dependence on each other that gives us a lump in our throats.

It is time to go, and for the children it is time for dinner. Watching them queuing excitedly outside the kitchen window and seeing them coming away chattering to each other with plates piled with good simple food, I know we are already in their past. And I know that we want more than anything else to be part of their future. Hopefully, through Toybox, we can.

time passes and they begin to trust, to establish relationships. They learn to be a child again.

The Fountain
and the Dance

The Fountain

 It was late afternoon on our last day in Lima, and there was still one project to visit. I really wished there wasn't. I was feeling very fed up. Foolishly, I had not been wearing a hat in the searing sun. As a consequence the skin on my cheeks and forehead and especially my nose was cooked. My face was one big red globe. Very funny for everyone else, no doubt, but very sore for me. In addition, like the rest of the team, I was exhausted. We had seen and done so many things on that long, long Monday and, as we got into our taxis to journey to El Niño Emanuel, I privately reckoned that this was one project too far. Closing my eyes as our taxi pulled out into this crazy pinball machine of a city that local drivers negotiated with varying degrees of expertise every day, I fantasized about returning to our hotel, our room, the shower, the change of clothes, the meal, the bed. It all seemed very distant.

And it was. Our journey through the darkening streets of Peru's capital city was a little rehearsal for eternity. I continually shifted in my seat with frustration. How *could* it be so far? How *could* it take so long? If it was taking all this time to get there, then – good heavens! – it would take the same amount of time to get back. I groaned inwardly. What did I care about children or projects or Toybox or any of the other things that were supposed to be so important? Nothing! That was the answer. Let them all go hang. All I wanted in the world was to be on the other side of my hotel room door.

And then there was the dust. The parts of Latin America that we had seen so far seemed to be covered in a thick layer of sallow dust. It was as though all the goodness and fertility of the soil had long ago been sucked out and used up, leaving only a yellowish, lifeless remnant. As our small convoy of two taxis climbed higher and higher along less and less level roads away from the centre of the city, there was something about the combination of fading light and dead earth that made me feel even more depressed.

We arrived at last. At least, they said we had arrived. When I finally managed to creak my way out of the low-roofed taxi all I could see was a

few tumbledown buildings, dust and yet more dust and, directly in front of us, two great big closed gates, made out of something like corrugated iron.

Sighing, I said to myself, 'Ah, well, let's get on with it. The sooner we do it the sooner we go home.'

We walked through the gates and stepped into a fountain. It was a fountain that, in an instant, washed away all my moaning and self-pity. There was no water in it. It was made of children. It was as though they had burst from the dust itself, full of colour and richness and refreshment. Each of us was festooned with little boys and girls, all displaying the instant unselfconscious affection that, as we increasingly discovered, is a genuine and wonderful feature of children in this part of the world. Afterwards I recorded in my notebook the fact that 'today we saw a galaxy of smiles.'

We were whirled around to see many, many things at El Niño Emanuel. The girls had the pinkest bedrooms you ever saw. The boys' dormitories were painted in a manly blue. There were classrooms, medical rooms, places to eat and places to play. Everything was vivid and colourful, a rainbow of an environment. And the children belonged. They owned their lives. It was their place.

My guide around the project was a stern little girl with shoulder-length brown hair and the expression of one who might one day become an international events manager. She was probably eight years old. What is it about me that causes small females to treat me as though I am a sort of last-ditch behavioural project? I must ask my daughter. This little girl took me by the hand and marched me round the various rooms, explaining their different functions in a language that I did not understand, fixing me with a very straight gaze every now and then to check that I was paying attention. Eventually, with no warning at all, she stopped, turned her face up towards mine and said, in clear English, 'Will you sponsor me?'

Ask me how I felt at that moment, and all I will be able to tell you is that when I did eventually get back to that blessed beacon of a hotel, I wrote this sad little poem.

A serious little girl asked me if I would sponsor her
And so I said no for all the best reasons
And so I didn't sponsor her
And so she isn't sponsored yet
And so there we are then
And so . . .
I wish I had sponsored her

She was a drop in that fountain that had burst from the dust and lifted me out of my dismal self. I pray that she and all the other little drops will find all they need and deserve in a future that will certainly be far from easy. I would hate for all that colour to go out of their lives.

The Dance

What impedes spiritual growth? I am not even sure what that question means any more, but I can tell you one thing. Many of the people I meet are more hopelessly shackled by their principles than by their sins.

I never do this.
I wouldn't do that.
I always do it in a particular way.
I could never bring myself to go there.
My principles wouldn't let me.
I wasn't brought up like that.

These atrophied moral fossils or fondly cherished certainties can be nothing more than defences against the threat of change and discomfort. Sometimes they are the sticking point in those tiny Gethsemanes that followers of Jesus face every day. Some you win, some you lose. I don't keep score, but so far the losses are definitely in the lead. Now, don't worry. I am not about to tell you of a major victory in my life. How could I, when I was more or less ambushed into doing what I did?

I never dance. Okay, it's not exactly a principle in the usual sense, but if you had ever seen me trying you might be forgiven for believing that, for

I hear a little
voice at the
back of my
mind feebly
calling out, 'Do
you realize
what you're
doing?

the sake of onlookers, it should be. Seriously, the whole thing terrifies me. Sometimes Bridget and I say prayers in which we announce to God that we are open to his guidance: ready and willing to go anywhere or do anything that is required of us. This is well-meant, arrant nonsense, as we all know, but sometimes we come close to thinking we really mean it. Always, though, always and every time, I insert a silent clause into the contract that reads simply: 'I shall not under any circumstances be required to dance.' In any case, I say to myself, how is anyone else ever going to genuinely benefit from the absurdity of me trying to dance? It's simply not going to happen.

Having said all this, I do need to point out something that I have mentioned many times in the past. You simply cannot trust God.

So, there I am at El Niño Emanuel, sitting in the big dining hall watching a succession of meticulously rehearsed dances performed to a backing track with great enthusiasm and skill by a group of little girls dressed in colourful national costume. We are all there, all the members of our little team, and each of us has a child or three leaning or sitting or hanging on to laps and arms and shoulders. We watch four of the dances, each involving a lot of charming smiles, teapot-posturing and head-wobbling. We love it, and I doubt if any of us has guessed what is about to happen as the fourth dance ends.

A new piece of music begins, and suddenly a prearranged plan explodes into action. Each of us finds both of our hands grasped by a child, and before we have time to react or respond we are on our feet and dancing. The whole room is filled with children and grown-ups and music and dance. Dazed by the speed and precision of this expertly choreographed *fait accompli*, I hear a little voice at the back of my mind feebly calling out, 'Do you realize what you're doing? You're dancing with children in a project somewhere on top of a dusty hill in Lima. You don't dance anywhere! Stop!'

But it was all right. It was all right for two reasons. The less important one was the fact that I could see my friend David Withers dancing just a few feet away from me. David is a truly wonderful person, but for someone like me the style and quality of his dancing was – how can I charitably express it? – reassuring. The second reason, more profound and much less definable, was a reminder that sacrifice and celebration get on awfully well together, just as repentance and joy become almost inseparable once they get to know each other.

My brief dance was not much of a Gethsemane, was it? I never actually made a decision. On the other hand, it reminds me of a crucial truth. I don't want to do all sorts of uncomfortable things, but most of all, as I have already said: I do not want to be a follower of Jesus who offers edited commitment. Of course, this is very much a work in progress, but at least it's *in* progress. A genuine desire to help the neglected children of Latin America will call for a depth of sacrifice and commitment that goes far beyond individual choices and preferences. Jesus invites us to take the hands of these children and move to the music of his love and compassion. Like most of us, I feel nervous and inadequate when this invitation arrives, but yes, however silly I look, I do want to be part of the dance.

The Good News

And lo, it came to pass that news of a strange and momentous happening, taking place in a far country, reached the ears of those who dwelt in the lands known as East Sussex in England.

No prophecy was fulfilled that day, for none had been foretold.

No earth shook, nor did floods cover the earth.

Yet the people of Emmanuel Church, Hailsham and the family of Plasses were sore amazed and cried as one,

"Tis surely a miracle!'

For on that precious day of January 2008, high in the hills overlooking the ancient city of Lima,

Adrian danced.

A Sign of Hope

Have you ever noticed our tendency to use the word 'hope' when we are, in fact, running out of hope? I grew up in Carlisle, in the north of England. When people say it rains a lot in the Lake District, they are not exaggerating. It rains *a lot*! I remember spending many a day standing in a tennis club shelter, staring gloomily out at the abandoned courts, and saying to my brother, 'I hope it stops raining soon.' We both knew it probably wouldn't.

When I met Nancy she used the word 'hope' in a very different way. She used it to refer to a very special person: her personal sign of hope – her three-week-old son, Isaiah Joshua. The birth of a first child can be emotional and exciting for all new parents, but for Nancy the arrival of Isaiah was significant for one major reason. He was born off the streets. This is something most people would take for granted, but, just six months earlier, the idea of her and her son being able to be anything other than yet another street family had seemed inconceivable. She told me that life had been a downwards spiral for such a long time that it seemed impossible for anything good to appear on the horizon. It would be foolish to hope it might, as she'd only face another disappointment, for time and again Nancy's hopes had been dashed and her dreams replaced by nightmares.

Fortunately for her, hope was just around the corner, springing up on her when she least expected it. With nowhere to live and no one to ask for help, Nancy had been forced to make the streets of La Paz her home. However, unbeknown to Nancy, who undoubtedly felt invisible and unimportant, the streets of La Paz were very much on the radar for a group of street workers who believe that people like Nancy deserve more.

They saw past the life she was currently leading. They saw beyond the begging and stealing, the alcoholism and despair, the lifestyle which would do anything for a bit of money or the chance of a hot meal and a bed for the night. They knew that this behaviour didn't need to define her life forever. There was much more to this young lady than a cursory glance might reveal. She had potential. She had a caring spirit. Behind the pain and anger in her eyes there was a child, longing to be loved, accepted and understood.

Believing life could be different was not easy for Nancy. But with the support and advice of the team around her, she gradually let her heart and mind explore a new path: one that allowed her to be important, to matter, and to be able to make different choices.

And, six months later, she is in so many ways unrecognizable from the woman she was before. As we sat with her and Isaiah, she carefully and quietly explained how her life had been completely turned around. She was now firmly established as one of the family in the Esperanza Viva rehabilitation centre she now called home. She was receiving counselling and support which had helped her to begin to address some of the pain of her past. She had begun to break free from her addictions and she was now able to allow herself to dream.

Some people say that the world's problems are too big, we can't make a difference. Try telling that to Nancy. She knows otherwise. On the streets, her pregnancy was yet another trauma and difficulty in her life. Six months on and she's now delighted by her young son Isaiah. As we watched her hold him in her arms we knew that we had witnessed another small victory in the quest for justice.

for Nancy the arrival of Isaiah was significant for one major reason. He was born off the streets.

A Gift Too Small?

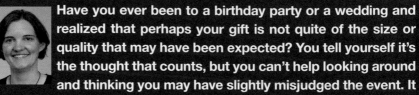

Have you ever been to a birthday party or a wedding and realized that perhaps your gift is not quite of the size or quality that may have been expected? You tell yourself it's the thought that counts, but you can't help looking around and thinking you may have slightly misjudged the event. It appears that your offering just doesn't quite match the rather more extravagant displays of your fellow partygoers. To make things worse, you offer your gift to the party host who acts as though he or she is overwhelmingly grateful. Inwardly you are squirming, sure that these outward signs of gratitude are simply covering up inner disappointment with your less than inspiring contribution.

I experienced very similar feelings during my visit to the Esperanza Viva project. The trip began like most other project visits. We were warmly welcomed and introduced to both the staff and those living within the project. We were able to chat to them about their lives, find out about the project and catch a glimpse of how things were going.

But not long into the visit, the project leader asked us to accompany him on a short tour of some of the rooms. We visited the small kitchen area where the food was prepared. The facilities were very basic but at least the team was able to provide a reasonable level of nutrition. I figured there wasn't much to look at here and expected us to be moved on very rapidly, but at that point, the leader gestured towards us, encouraging us to look at his collection of plastic cups, plates and bowls. I didn't really know what to say in response to his enthusiasm for what appeared to be just a giant picnic set. However, as I listened carefully to what he was trying to explain to me in Spanish, I realized that he was trying to communicate his immense gratitude to me for providing these items. It turned out that Toybox, the organization I represented, had given Esperanza Viva funding to purchase these items for his kitchen.

'They've made a huge difference to this project,' he explained to me. 'Before we had these things we would have to share all our food from the one big pan it was cooked in. We had no clean cups to serve water in. We were so grateful that we had some rice or beans to give to the children and families, but we longed for the day when we could serve our residents more effectively. Thanks to you, we can now do that. These cups, plates and bowls really have changed things here. Thank you so much.'

I figured there wasn't much to look at here . . .

I smiled and thanked him for showing me the kitchen, explaining we were pleased to have been able to help. But inside, I was feeling very uncomfortable at this slightly unexpected turn of events. To begin with, I felt uneasy that I was being thanked for the picnic set when it wasn't actually me who gave the money, but some other people back home, who no doubt will never know exactly what their money has been used for.

Also, and more significantly, I had a growing feeling within me that we really hadn't given enough. I was fairly sure that in my hotel room I had more than enough local currency to go out and buy more than just a giant plastic kitchen set. Here I was in the middle of so much need, being thanked so enthusiastically for some plastic items which were probably worth less than my friends and I might spend between us on a trip to the cinema and a pizza. The huge inequalities of the world suddenly hit me in a whole new way. The realities of my lifestyle versus the huge need before me were not something I could hide from. Here they were, plain to see, impossible to ignore.

> The huge inequalities of the world suddenly hit me in a whole new way.

I'm the type of person who loves solutions. If I see a problem, I want to work out how to fix it. I hate leaving things undone. I get frustrated if progress isn't being made. That applies to the small things in life but also to the big things I see. I look at the Esperanza Viva project and I see so much potential: so many things we could provide; so many ways we could improve life for the residents. But the people there aren't asking me to sort their project out for them. They are not expecting me to go in and fix every problem. I don't hold the key to their success. They've got that. They know where they are going. They know what their dream is. They're pressing on and they're making it happen.

Mother Teresa once said 'We ourselves feel that what we are doing is just a drop in the ocean. But the ocean would be less because of that missing drop.'

I may have stood in that small project in Bolivia and felt that our contribution was just a drop in the ocean. But that project would be less than it is today without that giant plastic picnic set!

Section Six
Young Ambassadors:
A Passion for Change

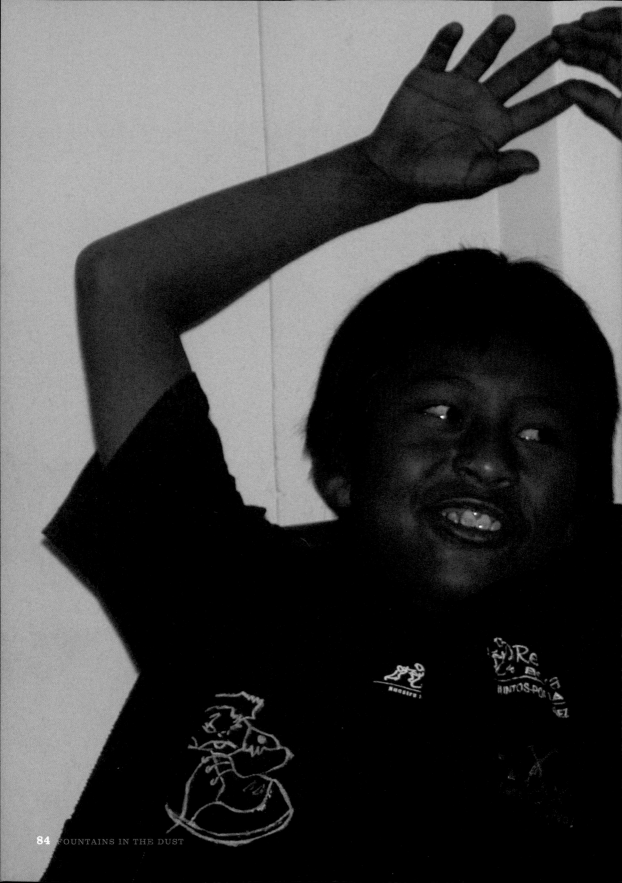

Briefings:
Child
Ambassadors

Each of the projects we visited in Bolivia had two child ambassadors.

These ambassadors were elected by a democratic ballot which all the children in their project took part in.

The ambassadors from all the projects in each town or city are gathered together at least once a month for training and to take part in activities.

They represent the children in their project. They provide feedback and advice to the project leaders. They work together to try to change things for the better in their own communities.

attention. Once they had an audience they were able to talk to people about what it means to treat children well. If people wanted to sign up to their good treatment campaign, they were given a little vaccination card which listed the positive things children need, things like a little bit of patience, a touch of humour and a lot of love. Once their vaccination card had been stamped by the children, they were also given a 'good treatment' sticker and a sweet to take away with them.

The ambassadors told us how nervous they had been as the vaccination day approached. However, the day was a fantastic success. The ambassadors were so proud of all they were able to achieve. In fact, they are so excited by what happened that day that they are planning many more vaccination campaigns in the future.

As I sat with the ambassadors in Cochabamba and listened to all they had to say, I reflected on the fact that we often talk about children as being the leaders of tomorrow. We justify our investment in their lives by saying that they are the future of the church, the future for our country and the future of the world. But, as I saw that day, this is not just about the future. Children and young people can also be the leaders of today. These ambassadors are so clearly demonstrating this through their efforts to bring about change. They've known what it is to suffer and to have to be silent about the things that matter. Now they've been given a voice and they're using it to bring about good.

'Our lives begin to end the day we become silent about things that matter' – Martin Luther King Jr.

Section Seven
Growing Up
Behind Bars

BRIEFINGS: PRISON IN BOLIVIA

When parents in Bolivia are sentenced to prison, many children find the prison becomes their home too.

An estimated 1,200 children currently live in prison in Bolivia.

Bolivian prisons are overflowing, with occupancy rates at around 164 per cent across the country.

Many prisoners are held for years without formal conviction. Food is scarce and medical provision almost non-existent.

Think Prison

Think Dickens. Think Oliver Twist. Think claustrophobic, irregularly shaped living spaces on crazily different levels. Think cardboard, scraps of wood, sheets of plastic and threadbare pieces of cloth employed as makeshift walls to divide you from your neighbour. Think long ranks of battery chickens, then replace the image of dumb, helpless creatures with men, women and children of all ages. Think the narrowest of narrow passages. Think eyes and faces appearing like strange, pale ghosts above your head as you negotiate the slit-like canyons of San Antonio prison. Think hopelessness. Think despair.

Prison Break

As I took my seat and glanced across the table, I had a feeling this was going to be a difficult conversation. I guess there was no reason to assume it wouldn't be. I was a foreigner. I was trying to negotiate, in my less than perfect Spanish, my way into San Antonio prison in Bolivia. Not only that, but I was trying to convince this slightly aggressive-looking prison governor that he'd really like to allow me, and my five British travelling companions with their cameras and notebooks, to take an unprecedented look at what was happening behind those prison gates which separated the outside from the inside world. Previous attempts had failed, but maybe this time we could obtain even the smallest of glimpses into the reality of life behind bars?

I can completely understand the governor's reluctance to grant our request. He spends most of his time preventing people from leaving the prison and now here he was trying to prevent people from entering. What were our motives? What could the consequences be?

We were all apprehensive about what we might encounter on the other side of those gates. But our motive for entering was to unearth more of the truth, to find out what life is like. Not just for the prisoners, although their experiences are part of the picture. But our primary focus that morning was to discover how this life treated children for whom the prison has become home. We had visited projects working to help children who live in prison, but without seeing where the children were coming from, the picture was incomplete.

Having explained our link to the prison projects and our ongoing commitment to supporting those projects in the years to come, the governor eventually conceded us access to the inside for an hour or so. I got the feeling he was taking great delight in making me work for that right to enter, and as he forced me to listen to his repeated lectures about prison life, I was very aware that each repetition was getting louder and louder. His eyes popped angrily at me and his skinny frame shook ever so slightly with rage. This was his prison, his territory. He was very much in control. I was just happy to see the gates opening and to find that we were being ushered in, albeit without our passports which were confiscated on the door!

It's worth noting that my male travelling companions had a more complicated entrance procedure than I did. Not only were their passports

removed from their possession, but they also had to have their hands stamped with a special symbol and code. This stamp indicated to the staff and security personnel that they were just visiting the prison. They were informed that they must not wash off the stamp during their visit. Women and children are free to leave the prison at any time but, as it was a male prison, any men wishing to leave had to prove their innocence by displaying their stamp. Clearly none of the men in our group were going to be washing their hands during our stay behind the main gate!

Whilst I may have been pleased to see the gates opening, that temporary feeling of relief was very quickly replaced by a whole range of other emotions as they slammed behind us, and the reality of life on the inside began to overwhelm us. My mental image of prison had been largely informed by film and TV images. The pictures that flooded my mind that morning were in no way similar to any of those preconceived ideas. Home to more than three hundred people, this prison was small, cramped and dingy. The cells weren't professionally constructed with metal bars. They'd been assembled from corrugated iron, wood, cardboard: anything that could provide some kind of structure and separation between the designated areas. Stacked up on top of each other, these cells were crammed in to maximum capacity.

Outdoor space was nearly non-existent and with only four showers between them all, there was a fairly strict bathroom rota required.

This is no place for children to be growing up, I thought to myself. The kids in here have done nothing to deserve a life behind bars. They are kids who just happen to have a parent who's been convicted of a crime and so their home has been moved from the outside to the inside.

Not surprisingly, as the people we talked to at the local project told us, an estimated seventy per cent of children living in prison end up on the streets if a prevention project doesn't step in to help them. The children aren't prisoners. They can come and go as they like. And, with a prison like this one as the only place they can call home, it's not surprising that a life of freedom on the outside would seem a better option. But is it?

The cells weren't professionally constructed with metal bars. They'd been assembled from corrugated iron, wood, cardboard: anything that could provide some kind of structure and separation

Karina and Fernando

 I first met Karina and Fernando in Oruro, a place that already seemed dark and strange to Bridget and me and the rest of the team. We had heard some alarming things about this ancient Bolivian city. The locals, we were told, believed that the devil owned all the mineral mines beneath the city, while God laid claim to everything above ground. Apparently the Roman Catholic church stood directly above one of these mines. Children as young as eleven and twelve were made to work in the mines and sleep next to images of the devil so that they would learn not to fear him.

As always in unfamiliar countries it was hard to know how much of this to believe, but it is worth recording that on our first night in the city we had watched a practice run for the forthcoming festival parade, when statues of mermaids, God and the devil would be carried through the streets as the people danced along behind. Images of God and the devil in the same parade? It made our flesh creep.

There was nothing creepy about the restaurant where we met Karina and Fernando. It was our second encounter with a group of ambassadors, and these kids, more than twenty of them seated on both sides of a long line of tables pushed together, were as lively and animated as the children we had met in Peru.

Much of the meal was taken up with an attempted exchange of humour. Would English jokes work in Bolivian Spanish, even after being passed through the filter of translation? What about the other way round? Gabriella, Ana Belen and Michael – three very bright ambassadors sitting across the table from Bridget and I – were as keen and determined to find out as we were. So here are two highlights.

Michael's joke was about a little cookie who ran around shouting boastfully, 'I'm a cookie! I'm a cookie! I'm a cookie!' Eventually the baker could stand it no longer. He took his gun and shot the middle right out of the cookie. Unabashed, the cookie continued to run around, but now he was shouting, 'I'm a doughnut! I'm a doughnut! I'm a doughnut!'

Hilarity reigned. Michael was, quite rightly, not at all modest.

Our contribution, announced by me as the best-known joke in the English language, was simple and predictable.

'Why did the chicken cross the road?'

There was something very vivid about the girl, not just the way she looked, but a burden of inner feeling, a weight of emotion.

Different culture. Different continent. Different context. Would they know the time-honoured response?

They did.

'To get to the other side!'

It was like a firework going off, so bright and loud and sparkly. The meal was a great occasion, very relaxed, easy to enjoy.

There were two slightly older children sitting further up the table, on the same side as our three little jokers. The girl was very dark with large expressive eyes and jet black hair swept across her forehead. The boy was a steady-looking individual with regular features, short brown hair and an air of quiet resilience. They interested me. Why? Don't know. There was something very vivid about the girl, not just the way she looked, but a burden of inner feeling, a weight of emotion. I thought I detected a bond between the two children that was almost visible. Changing places with someone on my side of the table, I sat opposite them. Our interpreter told me that their names were Fernando and Karina. They were fourteen years old.

'Where do you two live?' I asked.

A shadow passed across Karina's face. She threw a sideways glance at Fernando, and then gestured to right and left, indicating the rest of the children seated at the restaurant table as she spoke.

'She does not wish to say in front of the others,' said our interpreter, 'but she will tell you afterwards at the project office.'

I smiled and nodded, but inside I shivered as I had shivered on hearing about the children in the black mines of Oruro. I wanted to warn her, to tell her that it might be better not to say anything at all to us. I said nothing. What should I have done? Judge for yourselves.

The Interview

There are tears that gush noisily in sudden torrents of uncontrollable distress, and there are tears that seep from pools so full of sorrow that the slightest emotional tilt can cause them to brim over. These are the tears I am witnessing now, silently spilling over her lower lashes, slowly sliding down familiar tracks, making a detour past her nose and the corners of her quivering mouth, some captured by the back of her hand, the rest dripping onto the table in front of her.

It is not good. Ten minutes ago this fantastic fourteen-year-old girl was laughing and fooling around with the rest of her friends. Now she is sitting opposite us, her fellow ambassador next to her, struggling to share her story. Fernando, who joined in enthusiastically at first, is finding the whole experience too much and is sitting slumped forward, his head cushioned on his folded arms, eyes firmly shut. Karina is proving to be made of sterner stuff.

'My dad got divorced to my mum and he went away with my two big brothers so now I am the oldest. My mum had to go to prison and so I had to go with her to live there. I had to work a lot because I had to take care of my sisters. I also had to work hard to help my mother. Sometimes it is very hard.' Her voice catches. Traitorous tears threaten to betray her again. Sensing her embarrassment, Fernando turns his head, still on his hands, and looks at her for a moment. Straightening up abruptly he fishes into the sleeve of his anorak, extracts a small twist of crumpled pink toilet paper and passes it to her wordlessly before resuming his position of determined non-involvement. It is enough. She dabs at her face with the tissue and manages a watery smile.

'I have a little sister called Lilly Anna. She is five. I read her stories at bedtime. Red Riding Hood is her favourite. I have to be very aware. I do not want my sisters to end up living on the streets. Many children whose families live in prison end up on the streets. But right now,' she pauses, bites her lips, looks up to the ceiling and continues, 'Right now, I do not live in the prison with them.'

Karina goes on to tell us that at the moment she is living with an auntie but the auntie is shortly going away so she will be homeless.

'My project is trying to help me find me a house – somewhere I can live.'

I learn later that because she is doing so well at school, the project she represents, Angel House, is thinking of sending her to a residential home in Cochabamba where she can continue her studies. Real hope for the future for this intelligent teenager. But this will mean she will be far away from her mother and her sisters.

'I still don't know if I will be able to visit my mother – it is really hard to leave my friends and people I know here. My mother, she must stay in the prison for one more year.'

I think of her mother coping without her eldest daughter in the horrific cramped circumstances of a prison similar to the one we visited in Cochabamba and I shudder. I picture Lilly Anna longing for bedtime stories, puzzled as to where her big sister has gone. The sad truth is that Karina's future comes at incalculable cost to her little family still struggling inside prison. As tears start spilling over yet again, I know that Karina is thinking the same thing.

Sensing she has come to the end of her rope we steer the conversation on to what they both hope to be when they grow up. Fernando joins the conversation again, clearly very relieved it has moved onto safer ground.

'I would like,' he says with surprising authority, 'to help release prisoners because it is very dangerous inside the prison. Sometimes there are strikes and people fight and I have seen someone die. I do not think this is right.'

Karina takes the question equally seriously. She would like to help children in prison situations. Maybe become a policewoman but, she admits with a somewhat liquid smile, she hates the olive green uniform, so maybe she will be a children's doctor one day.

Both agree that their project helps them in many ways. Fernando tells us that in prison there is no provision at all for families.

'There is only food for the prisoner so children often don't eat. Our project provides food and school books and stops little children from being taken away to government homes where they are beaten and punished.'

Adrian prays with them. I proffer a bag of sweets and tell them to help themselves. Fernando takes a ridiculously large fistful with a grin so wicked and boyish I sense his recovery is only minutes away. Karina hangs back for a group hug but then she too rushes off to join her friends in preparing a drama for showing later in the afternoon, the lid firmly back on her tears until the next occasion when distraction will provide inadequate protection.

I am left angry and sore, hating myself and Adrian and everyone else involved in putting these children through this ordeal, but above all hating a world where innocent children have to bear the full weight of an unjust system.

> The sad truth is that Karina's future comes at incalculable cost to her little family still struggling inside prison.

A Wounded Bird

I killed a song thrush with an air pistol when I was nine years old. I think the pistol belonged to my older brother. I took it from his room and went out into the field near where we lived. I had a pocketful of pellets as well. I wanted to shoot something. I wanted to be like the cowboys in the films, using the power of my gun to dramatically affect a living creature.

I was a terrible shot, but I became wild and feverish with the desire to see a bird fall as a result of what I had done. Up and down the hedges I roamed, firing and missing again and again at sparrows and chaffinches and blackbirds. Finally, I hit something. A song thrush fell from the lowest branch of a small tree at the end of the field.

a child grown up before her time because of circumstances that are beyond her control.

It wasn't dead. Lying in the long grass it twitched and moved. I could see the frantic pumping of its heart. Creation froze. I froze. My blood seemed to freeze. What had I done? Terrible, terrible, terrible! I had hurt this poor bird for no reason at all. Now I would have to kill it to make the suffering stop. I must have fired three or four pellets into the soft, feathered form before the eyes filmed over and the body was still. I ran away from the dreadful scene, my eyes filled with tears. I never knowingly killed another living thing.

You have to be careful about this kind of driving intensity. It can happen at any time and take you in all sorts of directions. Here is an example.

You travel to a country like Bolivia to make a film and to collect stories and information about children in difficult circumstances. The trip goes well, except for the lack of a starkly dramatic moment, a revelation of personal suffering, real tears running down a real face because really bad things are being excavated and exposed. It could be a fourteen-year-old girl, for instance, a child grown up before her time because of circumstances that are beyond her control. She weeps. How can she not weep? One little verbal tilt is all that it takes.

Good stuff! Pens scratch across notebooks. Cameras feed hungrily on this rich visual fare. Now at last we have that essential nugget of live emotion that we were missing.

Of course, the comparison is not a fair one. There may have been a part of Karina that needed to release some of that pain. She was already injured. We just opened up the wound. Anyway, we are not nasty people: we are genuinely compassionate. In this case the ends might well justify the means. Lots of people will be moved by the sight of this child's agony and think seriously about giving money or time to the work of Toybox. That, after all, was the whole point of our trip.

All of these things may be true, but so is this. Before travelling to South America I had one memory of my own frozen guilt as I watched a helpless creature flutter to the ground. Now I have another.

Section Eight
The Rice Pudding Mystery

Briefings:
Prevention Work

Prevention is better than cure. This is why Toybox supports not only projects which work with children on the streets, but also those which are seeking to reduce the number of children taking to the streets in the first place.

These prevention projects typically work with the poorest children and their families in communities situated on the edge of the major towns and cities from which street children tend to originate.

Amongst other things, these projects provide food, education, advice and support. Project centres act as places of safety where children can be cared for, even if just for a day. In addition to this, social workers spend time in the community, visiting families and keeping an eye on those who are most at risk.

Paint Pots Full
of Happy Hope

'Happy Hope'. What a great name for a project! It was a project I'd heard of before I travelled to Bolivia but I had no idea what it really did.

As soon as we arrived we were lead into a large hall, crammed full of children. Loud music blared out from the speakers as the 240-strong choir enthusiastically sang and danced to the Christian choruses that were being played.

Having travelled to Latin American projects over a number of years I have got very used to arriving and joining in with whatever is going on. No need to ask questions, best just to dive in to whatever is on offer. And so, within minutes, I was standing near the back with a small collection of children, joining in the actions to the various songs and humming along to the tune.

A couple of songs later and it was time for something slightly quieter to happen. Although, as you can imagine, with 240 children in one hall nothing tends to be very quiet! As the traditional welcome speeches began, my eyes began to wander along the rows of children. I knew these were children who had to work to help their families and I began to consider what life must

be like for them outside the safety of this project. It was then that I began to notice something intriguing.

Each and every child seemed to have brought something with them. Some of the children retained a firm grasp of their item during the whole proceedings, whilst others kept theirs at their feet, presumably ready for when it was needed. They were all containers of one sort or another, but no two items seemed to be the same. Some children had

brought empty paint pots. Others had large brightly coloured buckets or small, dirty-looking cups. One girl had a little green jug. What, I wondered, was the purpose of this large array of receptacles? Had they been handed out for a game or craft activity? Were they props for a drama which we were about to be shown?

My ponderings were abruptly brought to an end as our little travelling group was invited to the front of the hall and we were asked to give our own speeches, something we became very used to as we ventured from place to place. A little later the speeches were over, the dances had been performed, the songs had been sung, the prayers had been prayed and it was time for us all to discover what was to become of the unusual collection of seemingly random items which continued to accompany these children wherever they went.

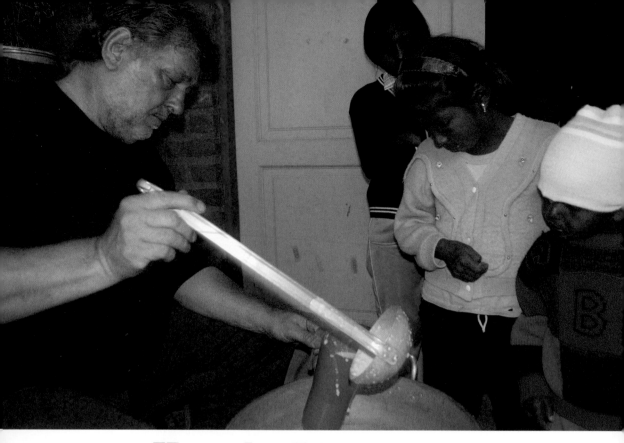

How the Rice Pudding Fed Me

I never actually consumed so much as a spoonful of rice pudding at the Happy Hope project, but in a funny sort of way, it fed me just the same. Bridget and I had been given a very simple job to do. In front of each of us, at opposite sides of the project building entrance, stood a huge metal saucepan of milky rice pudding. Herein lay the solution to Ange's puzzlement. Our task, using big, long-handled ladles, was to fill the extraordinarily wide selection of containers brought to us by an apparently endless line of children who had just been involved in the meeting. There were mugs and jugs and cups and buckets and vases and bowls of widely varying sizes. They were made of plastic and china and glass and pottery and wood and other vague substances that I was unable to identify.

Bridget and I had each been allocated a sharp-eyed umpire or judge. These unofficial officials stood beside us, checking that we did not fill vast

containers to the top, and that the much smaller ones were full to the brim. In addition they did their best to prevent villainous little individuals from emptying their rice pudding into a larger container elsewhere and then innocently turning up for a second or even a third helping. As far as we could see quite a number slipped through this net, one ubiquitous little green jug must have put in six or seven appearances on both sides of the door, but in the end there seemed to be plenty for all.

It was such a joy to do this. It really was. We were so thrilled to be allowed to supply nourishment to children who looked at their food as if they had been given a bucket heavy with diamonds rather than just a pint of sweet milky rice pudding. We were doing something instead of just watching: filling hungry children with food that was warm and good. Anyone could have done the job, but they didn't. We did. At one point Bridget and I looked up and smiled at each other across the doorway as we plied our ladles. God had appointed us as temporary milk monitors. We loved it.

And when you think about it, what more could you ask for from a Christian project? More than two hundred children, singing and dancing and playing games and eating rice pudding and being loved, and the whole thing being to do with Jesus.

> We were doing something instead of just watching: filling hungry children with food that was warm and good.

A Tale of Two Buildings

Buildings do not have huge expressive eyes or the gift of words to tell their story, but two buildings that we 'met' spoke so eloquently to me that they can't be excluded.

We had toiled our way up hundreds of crumbling stone steps, with only intermittent handrails to stop us from careering back down the steep uneven slopes. We had puffed and panted (well, Adrian and I had) and felt near to death. What kind of extraordinary experience would justify us being subjected to such an agonizing climb? I had thanked God over and over again for my replaced hip, without which I could never have got past the first twenty steps.

Finally we came to a halt outside – the public library?

Instantly banish your image of a tidy brick edifice with neat notice boards describing opening times, and a doorway leading to sound-deadened rooms containing rows of catalogued books, polished wood floors, children's cosy corners and efficient librarians. Replace that picture with a printed cardboard sign attached to a wobbly metal post, outside a minute wooden shack which appeared to be held together by wishful thinking, perched high up on the dusty barren hillside above Lima.

'Biblioteca Comunal'. An eloquent symbol of determination by the local pastor to give people who the world has forgotten a chance for their future. Inside the hut two beaming librarians proudly pointed out their somewhat ancient fluorescent light that hung crookedly from the rusting corrugated iron roof. Working electricity was clearly a luxury, even if the plastic cover was held together by gaffer tape. There was a small rack of children's books, a little row of reference books, another of novels, a few rather dirty, very well-thumbed periodicals, two tables to sit and read and study at, and a little line of coloured flags suspended across the ceiling. It was so beautiful and so hopeful that it actually made me want to cry.

Seeing this extraordinary library made me curious to meet the man whose vision had created such an inspiring place, and to visit his other building: the church, which was also located high on the hillside.

What kind of extraordinary experience would justify us being subjected to such an agonizing climb?

The Wise Man Built his House upon the Rock

Later that day, as dusk was falling and the crumbling poverty of the area was rendered almost beautiful by the sunset and twinkling lights far below us, we visited the pastor's church. He explained that he had been given an area of land on which to build a church, the only drawback being that it was literally a rocky section of very steep hill. First they had to hack out of the rock an area big enough to build on. Next they had to drag the huge boulders away and cover the flattish plateau they had made with concrete. Only then could they build their church, but, as they had no funding whatsoever, they had assembled an assortment of chipboard, wooden planks and corrugated iron, and cobbled them together, ignoring the inevitable gaps.

Already in awe of this man of God who was prepared to bring his vision to fruition in such a physical way, we entered the building. In front of us was a raised wooden platform. The pastor explained that some of the rocks had been hauled back inside and placed under the platform to give it support. On top of this were perched two wooden boxes, one on top of the other, covered with powder blue satiny cloth, flanked rather surprisingly by two huge vases of fresh flowers.

'The flower team have been busy today because we have just dedicated our new altar,' he explained proudly, pointing out the flower rota taped on the wall. Next to this were more rotas (well, you can't have a church without rotas, can you?) and a very strange ornate clock which had apparently been donated by a church in Japan. Nearby stood a dilapidated keyboard, a set of drums and cymbals for the music group, and what appeared to be an absolutely enormous modern sound system which turned out to be – an absolutely enormous modern sound system!

'It cost one and a half thousand dollars and it was given to us by a church on America. They also gave us these speakers,' he continued, pointing to two huge black boxes which we hadn't noticed until now.

Bearing in mind that the interior of the church measured no more than eighteen by twelve feet and the speakers could pump out enough volume to fill a concert hall, there was an unspoken question in all our minds.

Fortunately the pastor went on to explain,

'They also gave us loudspeakers to attach to the outside wall, along with the whole of the Bible on cassettes translated into our native language so that we can spread God's word all day and all night through our whole valley.'

Stunned into silence, we moved as one to the back of the church where a rickety table supported a Baby Belling single electric ring on which was perched a huge saucepan and piles of plastic mugs.

'We have so many hungry children here. On Sundays we feed sixty children with warm milk and give them bread. On special times we give them chocolate milk. Then we teach them about Jesus.'

'You are a fully trained pastor. Don't you ever wish you had a smart church in the centre of the city?' asked Adrian, in his innocently provocative way.

'Oh no,' he replied with a huge smile, 'There is far too much work for me to do here, especially with the children. We are a poor church but we believe children are not only our future: they are also God's gift to us. So we are planning to cut out some more of the hill to build them a little school, and we have made them a playground.'

It was getting almost too dark to see and we were all worrying about making our descent safely, so we said our goodbyes and gingerly tackled the downward journey back to the waiting van. On our way down we passed a group of children playing on the makeshift swings in their new playground. Looking back I could just make out the loudspeakers attached to the outside of the building.

Bumping along in the bus we discovered we were in agreement. Something was wrong with the balance. One and a half thousand dollars given to spread the good news by booming God's word to the poorest of the poor. No funding at all for spreading the good news by feeding children with warm milk and bread, teaching them about Jesus, building them a school with your bare hands and giving them somewhere safe to play.

That rickety little church may blow down at the first whiff of a storm, but we all agreed that this wise man had built God's house upon the deepest of foundations.

we can spread God's word all day and all night through our whole valley.

A Shed in the Middle of a Mess

 'Living Water'. There was an irony in the very title of the project. As we stepped gingerly down from the footplate of the splendidly clanking old bus that had been juddering our team around for the last few days, it was hard to believe that anything of value could be happening here. Rain had been falling heavily, turning the ever-present layer of dust into slippery yellow mud. The area in which we found ourselves was like a giant building site stretching away forever on all sides, littered with debris of various kinds and criss-crossed with furrows and ditches.

This stark, unwelcoming environment might have depressed us before we got started, but our brief experience of Bolivia was beginning to suggest that pearls of great price could often be found in very bleak fields.

Fifty yards away from the spot where our bus had come to a halt we could see an unevenly built brick building ringed with a narrow concrete path. Like some twenty-first-century ark on a raft, it stood in the midst of the yellow sea of sludge. This was our destination, the home of Living Water, yet another project dedicated to the task of rescuing children from the perils of life on the street. Making our way along a succession of carefully arranged but precariously balanced planks we finally managed to board the raft and enter the building.

The place was packed with life, bursting with children and a handful of workers. They looked relieved to see us. We were late. We were always late, everywhere we went. It seemed to be a fact of life in Latin America. Never mind. We were here now, and the programme that had been prepared for us could begin. Pictures from our time at Living Water are still in my mind.

I see the pastor who first envisioned this project. A thin, earnest man, he sits in the corner of the room by the door and tells us how he had always wanted to find a way to help children.

'For many years,' he says, 'I was waiting for God to act, and then I realized – I had to do something. Pastors should be pioneers of giving, and if what I do costs me nothing then it is not a sacrifice at all. We have had many problems. It was difficult to stop other people from getting the land

that we wanted and money has been short, but we are doing the work. This building is largely constructed of bricks discarded by builders. We have great needs. Our hope is that you do not see us as beggars. Scripture says that it is better to give than to receive, but to give is also a blessing and we must not take it away from the givers.'

As Bridget pointed out, this is by no means the first time that a building has been raised from the stones that the builders rejected.

I see six children, eyes bright with the contained excitement of public presentation as they rise to their feet and stand in a row with large placards held up for us to look at. Each card has different words written on it in big capital letters. The words are in English.

LAZINESS
JEALOUSY AND ENVY
LONELINESS
ANGER
VIOLENCE AGAINST THEM
HUNGER

These are the bad things these children have known in the past. We nod and smile our understanding and appreciation. There is a chorus of whispers and a great swishing and flapping as the placards are discarded and new ones are picked up. Smiles broaden. This is the really good bit. Now we are being shown words describing positive experiences that have replaced all those negatives because of the things that happen at Living Water.

HELP AND SUPPORT
TEAMWORK
WELLBEING
PARTNERSHIP
LOVE
RESPECT

We smile in return and clap appreciatively. Wonderful! Is that it? No, the children have one more set of cards to show us. This time they are really excited. We stare at the new set of cards in bewilderment for a moment. There is a single letter on each one. They must spell a single word. But what can XOBYOT possibly mean? Spanish? Martian? Sudden realization. Little

Little squeals and much shuffling of cards as the order is hastily reversed.

squeals and much shuffling of cards as the order is hastily reversed. That's better. TOYBOX. That's what it was supposed to say. Lots of laughter and prolonged applause. The overall message is clear:

'Thank you, Toybox, for helping to change our lives.'

I see Jenny and Jocelyn standing in front of us: graphic, living replies to any questions about why we should support work with street children in this part of the world.

Jenny is a full-time worker at the project. Small and bird-like, filled with passion, her eyes swim with tears as she talks about the feelings of inadequacy that have made it difficult for her to accept that she has a place here with these children who need so much care and support. Only last night, she says, God spoke to her and showed her that every time she hugs one of these little lost ones she is hugging Jesus. It is what she needed to know. She will stay and give herself to the work.

As she speaks, Jenny's arm is resting lightly across the shoulders of a slight little girl of seven or eight, a healed wound of a child with a dazzling smile. Her name is Jocelyn. Jenny tells us that all children are special, but there is something about Jocelyn's story that sums up the heart and spirit of Living Water.

Jocelyn was originally brought to the project by a neighbour. Her mother had died when she was very small, and her father had left home and disappeared not long after that. The grandparents reluctantly took her in. Jocelyn had never been to school. From the age of four she had been sent out at six o'clock each morning to the rubbish dumps to find plastic that could be sold for recycling. All she had to eat until four o'clock in the afternoon was a piece of dry bread. At first, in the project, this poor little scrap had simply been sad all the time. She was weak from lack of food

and emotionally flattened by lack of love and laughter. Now, three months later, there was flesh on her bones, she was playing with other children, and she had learned to smile. Project workers had spoken to her grandparents and helped them to understand that Jocelyn needed to be properly looked after.

It is not easy to describe the smile we saw on the face of this child. It was absolutely genuine, but it contained unmistakeable elements of both surprise and fear, surprise that things could have changed so suddenly and so wonderfully, fear that all these inexplicably beautiful things might simply dry up and blow away.

She need have no fear, but it will take much longer than three months for her to trust in her own good fortune.

Physically, Living Water is little more than a shed in the middle of a mess. In every other way it is one of heaven's outposts, a foxhole in no man's land, a place where children like Jocelyn, mere silhouettes of humanity, can be filled in and made whole and substantial by the divine artistry of reluctant heroes like Jenny.

Section Nine
Conclusions

days and weeks I've spent on the streets are so clearly some of the times in my life when I've felt my most alive and closest to God. Why? It's because in those times I'm so conscious of the heartbeat of God. I'm so acutely aware of what it is that matters in life. I know who I'm living for and I'm forced into a community situation where being isolated and individual doesn't work. I have to do life with God and with others.

This happens quite naturally when I work on the streets, but it doesn't have to stay there. Every time I leave I determine to live out some of those lessons when I get back home. But too often this desire to live differently doesn't tend to last for long. When I'm home, I'm so easily distracted by the cares and concerns of this world: some of them genuine, so many of them unnecessary.

> They steal my feeling of being alive.
> They take me out of community.
> I strive for independence.
> I become competitive.
> I'm driven by achievement.
> I lose my focus.
> I lose my dependence on God.
> I lose what really matters.

I had arrived at the home of Adrian and Bridget convinced I needed a sat-nav for my car. I left that afternoon aware that what I most needed was a sat-nav for my soul.

Giving to the poor is a fantastic thing to do. It changes lives. It changes communities. It honours God and it helps to unite the church around the world. But this was never meant to be a one-way thing. We may give to them financially but they have so much to teach us too.

> About values.
> About community.
> About dependence on God.
> About what really matters in this life.

It's not the big complicated concepts of our world. It's the simple stuff; the obvious stuff; the stuff which is so easily crowded out by the worries of this life. But embrace this and everything else begins to make sense.

Remaining Normal

Each time Adrian and I return from a trip to what we keep at arm's length by labelling the 'third world' we experience a huge sense of loss. Of course, it is nice to be home and see our family and friends and our dog. To have toilets that flush properly, ones where you don't have to put your used toilet paper into a bin to be collected and disposed of. To be able to cross the street without risking life and limb. To be able to drink water straight from the tap. To know that all dogs you meet are rabies-free. But nevertheless we always feel a bit cold and a bit depressed, and this time was no exception.

Coming home this time we realize it is the children themselves who we are missing. We spent such a fleeting time with them, but Michael's jokes, Maria Ruth's gently reproving frowns, Shirley's giggles, Richard's earnestness,

Karina's tears and Jocelyn's smile are just a few of the memory snapshots which we hope will never leave us.

A week or so after we had returned a friend of mine said, 'You must so wish you could bring them all back to England with you.'

Well, no, I don't!

If I am honest, while I value much about my country, I fear for our children's future. So many of them have lost their sense of purpose or any hope in their ability to change anything, and very few have a belief system which informs and influences their lives.

The children we met in Peru and Bolivia astounded us. It's not just their resilience to situations beyond our understanding, their confident faith, the personal courage they demonstrate in their ways of coping, or even that they turned out to be some of the most alert, intelligent and creative children we have had the privilege of meeting. It is that they have managed, against all reasonable odds, to remain normal.

Of course I want the personal circumstances of children in Latin America to be improved, but I would hate all these hard-won qualities to be corrupted. To see them lose the belief that through their actions the world can be a better place. To watch them lose their respect for teachers and their gratitude to those who are helping them. I would hate them to despise their education and lose sight of their goals in life, to become defined by their 'things', confused by choice, brutalized by media driven violence, rendered indifferent to the needs of those who don't quite fit into their own agenda. Many of our young people are losing the battle in these areas and I feel so sorry for them.

So, to the children we met in Latin America I would like to say,

'Stay there and grow strong through the love and commitment of all the servants of Jesus who have placed you into the centre of their lives. Become part of the fight against injustices in the system, part of the rescue package for children like yourselves who need your help. Grow in your faith and may God your Father bless you and keep you safe – oh, and please, please, let us help you.'

May God your Father bless you and keep you safe – oh, and please, please, let us help you.

Communion of Lights

On our last evening in Oruro we took over most of the top floor of a restaurant, to meet with all the pastors and workers who are linked with Toybox through various projects. There were many speeches, one or two songs, exchanging of gifts, and even (eventually) some eating.

For me, the highlight of the evening was the moment when each of us was given a candle, the lights were dimmed, and, one by one, we received and passed on the flame from our neighbour's candle, until the whole table was ringed with flickering light. This communion of lights seemed to encapsulate everything that is good and right, not just about this trip, but about followers of Jesus doing their very best wherever they are in the world.

Communion of Lights

We couldn't hold a candle to those people
But we did exactly that
One night in dark Oruro where the devil steals the name of God
And followers of Jesus battle day and night
To save the light that can so quickly die in children's eyes
We asked for darkness so that each of us
Could light a candle from our neighbour's flame
They flickered sometimes; some went out and had to be relit
It made us laugh, and that was fine
Laughter is a kind of prayer, an incense of the heart
I think it charms the one who came to light the world
The one who set a child apart
To show we should receive the truth with open eyes and innocence
The truth we learned that evening seemed to shine
And will do in the darkest caverns of so many other nights
Heaven will inhabit our communion of lights

Adrian Plass